THE
FACE
OF
CHRISTIANITY

Dr. Anthony Martin

Author ~ Scholarship ~ Leadership

Motivational Speaker

BEING BOUND
TO
CESARE BORGIA

The Kingdom Culture Fellowship Ministries
&
Christian Self Publishing's

This Book is dedicated to:

THE
SPIRITUAL
AWAKENING

THOSE WHO LOOK OUTSIDE

DREAMS

THOSE WHO LOOK INSIDE

IS AWAKEN

Content

THE

CHRISTIAN BLACK CODES OF

1724

To regulate relations between slaves and colonists, the Louisiana Code noir, or slave code, based largely on that compiled in 1685 for the French Caribbean colonies, was introduced in 1724 and remained in force until the United States took possession of Louisiana in 1803. The Code's 54 articles regulated the status of slaves and free blacks, as well as relations between masters and slaves.

Article I

Decrees the expulsion of Jews from the colony.

Article II

Makes it imperative on masters to impart religious instruction to their slaves.

Article III

Permits the exercise of the Roman Catholic creed only. Every other mode of worship is prohibited.

Article IV

Negroes placed under the direction or supervision of any other person than a Catholic, are liable to confiscation.

Article V

Sundays and holidays are to be strictly observed. All negroes found at work on these days are to be confiscated.

Article VI

We forbid our white subjects, of both sexes, to marry with the blacks, under the penalty of being fined and subjected to some other arbitrary punishment. We forbid all curates, priests, or missionaries of our secular or regular clergy, and even our chaplains in our navy to sanction such marriages. We also forbid all our white subjects, and even the manumitted or free-born blacks, to live in a state of concubinage with blacks. Should there be any issue from this kind of intercourse, it is our will that the person so offending, and the master of the slave, should pay each a fine of three hundred livres. Should said issue be the result of the concubinage of the master with his slave, said master shall not only pay the fine, but be deprived of the slave and of the children, who shall be adjudged to the hospital of the locality, and said slaves shall be forever incapable of being set free. But should this illicit intercourse have existed between a free black and his slave, when said free black had no legitimate wife, and should said black marry said slave according to the forms prescribed by the church, said slave shall be thereby set free, and the children shall also become free and legitimate; and in such a case, there shall be no application of the penalties mentioned in the present

Article VII

The ceremonies and forms prescribed by the ordinance of Blois, and by the edict of 1639, for marriages, shall be observed both with regard to free persons and to slaves. But the consent of the father and mother of the slave is not necessary; that of the master shall be the only one required.

Article VIII

We forbid all curates to proceed to effect marriages between slaves without proof of the consent of their masters; and we also forbid all masters to force their slaves into any marriage against their will.

Article IX

Children, issued from the marriage of slaves, shall follow the condition of their parents, and shall belong to the master of the wife and not of the husband, if the husband and wife have different masters.

Article X

If the husband be a slave, and the wife a free woman, it is our will that their children, of whatever sex they may be, shall share the condition of their mother, and be as free as she, notwithstanding the servitude of their father; and if the father be free and the mother a slave, the children shall all be slaves.

Article XI

Masters shall have their Christian slaves buried in consecrated ground.

Article XII

We forbid slaves to carry offensive weapons or heavy sticks, under the penalty of being whipped, and of having said weapons confiscated for the benefit of the person seizing the same. An exception is made in favor of those slaves who are sent a hunting or a shooting by their masters, and who carry with them a written permission to that effect, or are designated by some known mark or badge.

Article XIII

We forbid slaves belonging to different masters to gather in crowds either by day or by night, under the pretext of a wedding, or for any other cause, either at the dwelling or on the grounds of one of their masters, or elsewhere, and much less on the highways or in secluded places, under the penalty of corporal punishment, which shall not be less than the whip. In case of frequent offences of the kind, the offenders shall be branded with the mark of the flower de luce, and should there be aggravating circumstances, capital punishment may be applied, at the discretion of our judges. We command all our subjects, be they officers or not, to seize all such offenders, to arrest and conduct them to prison, although there should be no judgment against them.

Article XIV

Masters who shall be convicted of having permitted or tolerated such gatherings as aforesaid, composed of other slaves than their own, shall be sentenced, individually, to indemnify their neighbors for the damages occasioned by said gatherings, and to pay, for the first time, a fine of thirty livres, and double that sum on the repetition of the offence.

Article XV

We forbid negroes to sell any commodities, provisions, or produce of any kind, without the written permission of their masters, or without wearing their known marks or badges, and any persons purchasing any thing from negroes in violence of this article, shall be sentenced to pay a fine of 1500 livres.

Article XVI, XVII, XVIII, XIX

provide at length for the clothing of slaves and for their subsistence.

Article XX

Slaves who shall not be properly fed, clad, and provided for by their masters, may give information thereof to the attorney-general of the Superior Council, or to all the officers of an inferior jurisdiction, and may put the written exposition of their wrongs into their hands; upon which information, and even ex officio, shall the information come from another quarter; the attorney-general shall prosecute said masters without charging any cost to the complainant. It is our will that this regulation be observed in all accusations for crimes or barbarous and inhuman treatment brought by slaves against their masters.

Article XXI

Slave who are disabled from working, either by old age, disease or otherwise, be the disease in- curable or not, shall be fed and provided for by their master; and in case they should have been abandoned by said masters, said slave shall be adjudged to the nearest hospital, to which said master shall be obliged to pay eight cents a day for the food, and maintenance of each one of these slaves; and for the payment of this sum, said hospital shall have a lien on the plantation of the masters.

Article XXII

We declare that slaves have no right of any kind of property but that all that they acquire either by their own industry, or by the ability of others, or by any other means or title whatever shall be the full property but that all that they acquire either by their own industry, or by the ability of others, or by any other means or title whatever shall be the full property of their masters; and the children of said slaves, their fathers, mothers, their kindred or other relation either free or slave shall have no pretensions or claim thereto, either through testamentary nor positions or donations inter vivos; which dispositions and donations we declare null and void, and also whatever promise they may have interred into by persons incapable of disposing of anything and or participating to any contract.

Article XXIII

Masters shall be responsible for what their slaves have done by their command, and also for what transactions they have permitted their slaves to do in their shops, in the particular line of commerce with whom they were entrusted; and in case said slave should have acted without the order or authorization of their masters, said masters shall be responsible only for so much as has turned to their profit; and if said masters have not profited by the dining or transaction of their slaves, the per curium which the masters have permitted the slave to own, shall be subjected to all claims against said slaves, after deduction made by the masters of what may be due to them; and if said per curium should consist in whole or in part of merchandises in which the slaves had permission to traffic, the masters shall only come in for their share in common with the other creditors.

Article XXIV

Slave shall be incapable of all public functions, and of being constituted agents for any other person than their own masters, with powers to manage or conduct any kind of trade; nor can they serve as arbitrators or experts; nor shall they be called to give their testimony either in civil or in criminal cases, except when it shall be a matter of necessity, and only in default of white people; but in no case shall they be permitted to serve as witness either for or against their masters.

Article XXV

Slaves shall never be parties to civil suits either as plaintiffs or defendants, nor shall they be allowed to appear as complainants in criminal cases, but their master shall have the right to act for them in civil matters, and in criminal ones, to demand punishment and reparation for such outrages and excesses as their slaves may have suffered from.

Article XXVI

Slaves may be prosecuted criminally, without their masters being made parties to the trial, except they should be indicted as accomplices; and said slaves shall be tried at first by the judges of ordinary jurisdiction if there be any and on appeal by the Superior Council with the same rules, formalities, and proceedings observed for free persons save the exceptions mentioned hereafter.

Article XXVII

The slave who, having struck his master, his mistress, or the husband of his mistress or their children, shall have produced a bruise or the shedding of blood in the face, shall suffer capital punishment.

Article XXVIII

With regard to outrages or acts of violence committed by slaves against free persons, it is our will that they be punished with severity, and even with death, should the case require it.

Article XXIX

Thefts of importance, and even the stealing of horses, mares, mules, oxen, or cows, when executed by slaves or manumitted persons, shall make the offender liable to corporal, and even to capital punishment, according to the circumstances of the case.

Article XXX

The stealing of sheep, goats, hogs, poultry, grain, fodder, peas, beans, or other vegetables, produce, or provisions, when committed by slaves, shall be punished according to the circumstances of the case ; and the judges may sentence them, if necessary, to be whipped by the public executioner, and branded with the mark of the flower de luce.

Article XXXI

In cases of thefts committed or damages done by their slaves, masters, besides the corporal punishment inflicted on their slaves, shall be bound to make amends for the injuries resulting from the acts of said slaves, unless they prefer abandoning them to the sufferer. They shall be bound so to make their choice, in three days from the time of the conviction of the negroes ; if not, this privilege shall be forever forfeited.

Article XXXII

The runaway slave, who shall continue to be so for one month from the day of his being denounced to the officers of justice, shall have his ears cut off, and shall be branded with the flower de luce on the shoulder : and on a second offence of the same nature, persisted in during one month from the day of his being denounced, he shall be hamstrung and be marked with the flower de luce on the other shoulder. On the third offence he shall suffer death.

Article XXXIII

Slaves who shall have made themselves liable to the penalty of the whip, the flower de luce brand, and ear cutting, shall be tried in the last resort, by the ordinary judges of the inferior court, and shall undergo the sentence passed upon them without there being an appeal to the Superior Council, in confirmation or reversal of judgment, notwithstanding the article 26th of the present code, which shall be applicable only to those judgments in which the slave convicted is sentenced to be hamstrung or to suffer death.

Article XXXIV

Freed or born-free negroes, who shall have afforded refuge in their house to fugitive slaves, shall be sentenced to pay to the masters of said slaves, the sum of thirty livres a day for every day during which they shall have concealed said fugitives; and all other free persons, guilty of the same offense, shall pay a fine of ten livres a day as aforesaid; and should the freed or free-born negroes not be able to pay the fine herein specified, they shall be reduced to the condition of slaves, and be sold as such. Should the price of the sale exceed the sum mentioned in the judgment, the surplus shall be delivered to the hospital.

Article XXXV

We permit our subjects in this colony, who may have slaves concealed in any place whatever, to have them sought after by such person and in such a way s they deem proper, so to proceed themselves to such research as they may think best.

Article XXXVI

The slave who is sentenced to suffer death on the denunciation of his mater, shall, when that master is not an accomplice to the crime, be appraised before his execution by two of the principal inhabitants of the locality, who shall be especially appointed by the judge, and the amount of said appraisement shall be paid to the master. To raise this sum, and shall be collected by the persons invested with that authority.

Article XXXVII

We forbid all the officers of the Superior Council, and all our other officers of the justice in the colony to take any fees or receive any perquisites in criminal suits against slaves, under the penalty, in so doing of, being dealt with as guilty of extortion.

Article XXXVIII

We also forbid all our subjects in this colony, whatever their condition or rank may be, to apply, on their own private authority, the rack to their slaves, under any pretense whatever, and to mutilate said slaves in any one of their limbs, or in any part of their bodies, under the penalty of confiscation of said slave; and masters, so offending, shall be liable to a criminal prosecution. We only permit, masters, when they shall think that the case requires it, to put their slaves in irons and to have them whipped with rods or ropes.

Article XXXIX

We command our officers of justice in this colony to institute criminal process against masters and overseers who shall have killed or mutilated their slaves, when in their power and under their supervision, and to punish said murder according to the atrocity of the circumstances; and incase the offense shall be a pardonable one, we permit them to pardon said master and overseer without it being necessary to obtain from us letter patent of pardon.

Article XL

Slaves shall be held in law as movables, and as such, they shall be part of the community of ac-quests between husband and wife; they shall be seized under any mortgage whatever; and they shall be equally divided among the co-heirs without admitting from any one of said heirs any claim founded on preciput or right of primogeniture, or dowry.

Article XLI, XLII

Are entirely relative to judicial forms and proceedings.

Article XLIII

Husbands and wives shall not be seized and sold separately when belonging to the same master, and their children, who under fourteen years of age, shall not be separated from their parents and such seizures and sales shall be null and void. The present article shall apply to voluntary sales, and in such case sales should take place in violation of the law, the seller shall be deprived of the slave he has illegally retained and said slave shall be adjudged to the purchased without any additional price being required.

Article XLIV

Slaves fourteen years old, and from this age up to sixty, who are settled on lands and plantations, and are at present working on them, shall not be liable to seizure for debt, except for what may be due out of the purchase money agreed to be paid for them unless said grounds or plantations should also be distressed, and seized and judicial sale of a real estate, without including the slaves of the aforesaid age who are part of said estate, shall be deemed null and void.

Article XLV, XLVI, XLVII, XLVIII, XLIX

Are relative to certain formalities to be observed in judicial proceedings.

Article L

Master, when twenty-five years old, shall have the power to manumit their slaves, either by testamentary dispositions, or by acts inter vivos, but as there may be mercenary masters disposed to set a price on the liberation of the liberation of their slaves; and whereas slaves with a view to acquire the necessary means to purchase their freedom, may be tempted to commit theft or deeds of plunder, no person, whatever may he his rank and condition, shall be permitted to set free his slaves, without the obtaining from the Superior Council a decree of permission to that effect; which permission shall be granted without costs when the motive for the setting free of said slaves as specified in the petition of the master, shall, appear legitimate to the tribunal. All future acts for the emancipation of the slaves freed shall not be entitled to their freedom; they shall be taken away from their former masters, and confiscated for the benefit of the India company.

Article LI

However, should slaves be appointed by their masters tutors to their children, said slaves shall be held and regarded as being set free to all intent and purposes.

Article LII

We declare that the acts for the enfranchisement of slaves, passed according to the forms above described, shall be equivalent o an act of naturalization, when said slaves are not born in our colony of Louisiana, and they shall enjoy all the rights and privileges inherent to our subjects born in our kingdoms, or in any land or colony under dominion. We declare, however, that all manumitted slaves, and all free-born negroes are incapable of receiving donations, either by testamentary dispositions or by acts inter vivos from the whites. Said donations shall be null and void, and the objects of said donations shall be applied to the benefits of the nearest hospital.

Article LIII

We commend all manumitted slaves to show the profoundest respect to their former masters, to their widows and children, and any injury or insult offered by said manumitted slaves to their former masters, their widows or children, shall be punished with more severity than if it had been offered to any other person.

We, however declared them exempt from the discharge of all duties or services, and from payment of all taxes or fees, or anything else in relation to their person, or to their personal or real estate, either during the life or after the death of said slave.

Article LIV

We grant manumitted slaves the same rights, privileges, and immunities which are enjoyed by free born persons. It is our pleasure that their merit in having acquired their freedom, shall pro-duce in their favor not only with regards to their persons, but also to their property, the same effects which our other subjects derive from the happy circumstance of their having been born free.

In the name of the King,

Bienville, De la Chaise.

Fazende, Bruslé, Perry, March, 1724.

BEING BOUND TO CESARE BORGIA

Cesare Borgia is in the book entitled Triptych of Poisoners, and is also in the book entitled Cesare Borgia His Life and Times by Sarah Bradford. Between 1502 and 1503, he employed Leonardo da Vinci as a military architect and engineer in which him and Leonardo da Vinci became intimate instantaneously, they were lovers. To express his love towards Cesare, Leonardo painted many pictures of him. Cesare's Father Rodrigo Borgia, who later became Pope Alexander VI, under the authority of the Catholic Church Elite, had his son picture put up as Jesus Christ in the Western World. Cesare had sex with his own sister Lucrezia, and he killed his brother Giovanni in 1497, and this is the man whom the Catholic Church gave their consent to allowing his picture to be put up and portrayed as Jesus Christ to deceive the whole world to think Christ was European. See what most people don't know is, there was a competition during the time called the Renaissance period, between Leonardo da Vinci and the well known Michelangelo. The competition was to see who could impress the king by a making a new image of the King's son that would deceive the world, in which Leonardo da Vinci won the competition. The original King James Bible of 1611 had the Apocrypha in it, but in 1928 under the Vatican, they made an agreement to take 14 books out of the King James holy bible. Why you might ask, well because thousands of years before they put this image up to be Christ, they found out that it was written off in the Wisdom of Solomon located in the Apocrypha, that they would do this and the reason for it. So knowing this was written off in the Wisdom of Solomon, the Roman Catholic Church took it out of the bible so the people wouldn't figure out their deception. It is a noted fact that when they did this, they knew exactly what Christ people really looked like, they knew Christ and his people were not Europeans, but instead were actually Hebrews, who were dark brown people. So let's find out in the bible first what Satan was going to do, and then will find out what exactly was written in the Wisdom of Solomon that the Apocrypha had to be taken out and credited as unscriptural and not divinely inspired, by the Catholic Church. So what is written off in the bible that Satan would do? Revelation 12:9; And the great dragon was cast out, that old serpent, called the Devil, and Satan, which deceived the whole world: he was cast out into the earth, and his angels were cast out with him.

So it is written that Satan would deceive the whole world, in which he is doing this through the Catholic Church and through the so called children of God called the Jews, who are really the children of Satan according to Revelation 2:9 and 3:9. So now we know Satan plan is to deceive the whole world and we know that through the Catholic Church and the so called Jews are whom he is using to execute his plan. So now let's examine what was written in the Apocrypha that was so critical to our knowledge, that it had to be taken out and defamed as being unbiblical and not divinely inspired. This image that we see is said to be Christ and is portrayed all over the world as Christ, but says the word of God about it? Wisdom of Solomon 14:8; But that which is made with hands is cursed, as well it, as he that made it: he, because he made it; and it, because, being corruptible, it was called god. Scripture says that which is made with hands is cursed, but why would it be so? Isaiah 2:8; Their land also is full of idols; they worship the work of their own hands, that which their own fingers have made: Because the image that they put up, they called it Christ, which therefore it not being Christ made it a curse and a sin unto them because they themselves made it with their own hands and fingers. So therefore by calling it Christ, they give glory unto another and not the true and living God, therefore they worship it and give honor to it as being God which makes it idolatry. So being corruptible, this image was called God, so when the true people would begin to desire to learn about Christ, they would be told they worship this guy, then they would ask who is he, and they would be told he's Christ. What else is written? Wisdom of Solomon 14:9; For the ungodly and his ungodliness are both alike hateful unto God. Wisdom of Solomon 14:10; For that which is made shall be punished together with him that made it. So the image that the Catholic Church allowed to be put up as Christ will be destroyed, and also them and everyone who had a hand in pushing this deception unto the people, so there is a judgment awaiting them. They didn't do this to be nice, they had a motive behind pushing this deception which was mentally driving them to push a belief into the mindset of the people, in which they were pushing this during the Renaissance period. So now knowing that this image is idolatry and an idol of the heathens, what else is written about this? Wisdom of Solomon 14:11; Therefore even upon the idols of the Gentiles shall there be a visitation: because in the creature of God they are become an abomination, and stumbling blocks to the souls of men, and a snare to the feet of the unwise.

So by them doing this, they are an abomination unto God because in doing so, this image would become a stumbling block to the souls of men, and a snare to the feet of the unwise, how so? Because they knew Christ and his people wasn't European, so they knew that if they put up images of European people, then the true people would think the images are actually the people they are reading of in the bible. They knew they would open their bibles and see all these images of people who didn't resemble their skin color, but yet would see their family following this man who is suppose to be Christ, and see them believing that the people in these images were actually the people of Christ, and would feel excluded from the bible. So then they knew the true people would vary away from the bible and lose interest in it because they would consider it to be the white's man book, which this was part of their plan it's psychology at its best form. Because without a race having any biblical connection to coincide with their spirituality, they therefore will have no identity which would reverse their perception of self into a form of hatred towards others of their skin tone. Which is why black on black crime is high, because they can't look at each other and see they are one, which is also why our people learn to hate themselves and fight each other, but love all those who hate them, thus creating a stumbling block to the souls of men. So in the creation of this image and other images portraying Christ and his people as European, what came from this? Wisdom of Solomon 14:12; For the devising of idols was the beginning of spiritual fornication, and the invention of them the corruption of life. Wisdom of Solomon 14:13 - For neither were they from the beginning, neither shall they be forever. So in creating the false images of Christ and his people as Europeans, and worshipping them as Christ and his people doing so was the beginning of spiritual fornication. Why, because now when the people are not yet of Christ but learning of him, they are actually loving other gods whom the people aren't espoused to, so therefore they cheating on the true Christ with other gods spiritually, because they giving them time and love and affection and praise and worship as if they are the true Christ. But these images weren't here in the beginning, and neither shall they remain upon the earth forever. So how did these false images get here?

Introduction

The Apocrypha Book Wisdom of Solomon

Wisdom of Solomon 14:14 - For by the vain glory of men they entered into the world, and therefore shall they come shortly to an end. Scripture says by the vain glory of men these images entered into the world, and surely they shall soon come to amend in this world. So where does Cesare Borgia and his father Rodrigo Borgia come in the picture? Wisdom of Solomon 14:15; For a father afflicted with untimely mourning, when he hath made an image of his child soon taken away, now honored him as a god, which was then a dead man, and delivered to those that were under him ceremonies and sacrifices. Reference to his son Cesare, image put up to be Christ, which is how they honored him as a God though he was unknown at the time in Rome, thus making him dead. They used this false image of Cesare as Christ, and they brought forth a false teaching and ceremonies and sacrifices and holidays all along with this image, to deceive the people to believe these things were of this guy whom they were portraying as Christ. So what else came along with this the false Christ? Wisdom of Solomon 14:16; Thus in process of time an ungodly custom grown strong was kept as a law, and graven images were worshipped by the commandments of kings. From this false image, an ungodly custom grown strong was kept as a law, and that custom was Christmas, in which they told you it was the birthday of Christ. And they made Jesus pictures and Mary pictures and crosses and all forms of idolatry to resemble biblical things to appear European to support their demonic intentions. What else is written?

Wisdom of Solomon 14:17; Whom men could not honor in presence, because they dwelt far off, they took the counterfeit of his visage from far, and made an express image of a king whom they honored, to the end that by this their forwardness they might flatter him that was absent, as if he were present. Not everybody could honor this guy in the image as Christ in person, because some of the people lived far away. So they took this false image of Christ back to their native lands with them, and they made unto themselves images of other gods whom they could honor closely, so that they may worship their respective god in the images as if they were present. What did the people do? 2 Kings 17:29. Howbeit every nation made gods of their own, and put them in the houses of the high places which the Samaritans had made, every nation in their cities wherein they dwelt. Proved that!

Question: What else is written? Wisdom of Solomon 14:18 - Also the singular diligence of the artificer did help to set forward the ignorant to more superstition. Wisdom of Solomon 14:19 - For he, peradventure willing to please one in authority, forced all his skill to make the resemblance of the best fashion. Now remember the competition during the time called the Renaissance period, between Leonardo da Vinci and the well known Michelangelo, was to see who could impress the king by a making a new image of the King's son that would deceive the world, in which Leonardo da Vinci won. So by him winning and creating with his hands this false image of Christ, he set forward those who had no knowledge of this, meaning he caused them to have an irrational belief arising from ignorance of not knowing who this guy is that they are really worshipping. So Leonardo being willing to please Rodrigo Borgia, the Pope in authority at the time also the father of Cesare Borgia, he compelled all this talent to make the image resemble his son Cesare Borgia in the best way possible. What else is written?

Wisdom of Solomon 14:20; And so the multitude, allured by the grace of the work, took him now for a god, which a little before was but honored. Wisdom of Solomon 14:21; And this was an occasion to deceive the world: for men, serving either calamity or tyranny, did ascribe unto stones and stocks the incommunicable name. So after impressing him, the multitude of people were drawn by the elegance and beauty of this image and accepted it and took it to be their God, which beforehand wasn't revered by all as a God. And the reason they did this, was to deceive the world, and men begin to attribute this image and give credit to it, by not revealing to others who this guy is that's suppose to be God, thus fulfilling Revelation 12:9; And the great dragon was cast out, that old serpent, called the Devil, and Satan, which deceives the whole world: he was cast out into the earth, and his angels were cast out with him.

So Satan with the help of the Catholic Church has deceived the whole world into thinking this image is Christ, when it's really Cesare Borgia. What did Satan say? Isaiah 14:14; I will ascend above the heights of the clouds; I will be like the most High. So through this false image of Christ, Satan gets the glory as if he was God, like he said. So now you see why the Catholic Church took the Apocrypha out of the holy bible, they didn't want to get exposed, but It would come out one day.

Introduction

The whole world is deceived, they got this image on movies, cds and dvds, t-shirts, key chains, necklaces, bracelets, ornaments, stockings, pictures, coffee mugs, pens, air fresheners, wrist bands, watches, rugs, bill boards, windows, and even tattooed on their body, thinking it's Christ when really it's Cesare Borgia. So what should the people know and do? Deuteronomy 4:15; Take therefore good heed to yourselves; for you saw no manner of similitude on the day that the LORD spoke to you in Horeb out of the midst of the fire: Ask yourself, if the people didn't see no image of Christ, but only heard the voice of the words, then how did they know what he looked like? Yet, the images that were given by the Catholic Church are supposed to be Christ, but yet they don't look as how the bible says Christ looked. Why should they take good heed, what if they make them a similitude and say it's Christ? Deuteronomy 4:16; Less you corrupt yourselves, and make you a graven image, the similitude of any figure, the likeness of male or female, Deuteronomy 4:15 warned us to take heed because we never saw what Christ looked like, and Deuteronomy 4:16 tells us why, because of the making of an graven image, the similitude of any figure, the likeness of male or female. What is a graven image? Graven Image - a material effigy that is worshipped as a god. So those who have the blonde hair blue eyed picture who is suppose to be Christ, and those who have the black face dredlock hair picture who is suppose to be Christ, and those who have any picture that is supposed to be Christ, you are corrupted and an idolatry worshipper. Bible describes Christ and his people as people of color, but that doesn't give no one the right to make an image of what the bible says they look like. Repent before you burn in hell! Question: What else does the scripture say? 1 John 4:12; No man hath seen God at any time. If we love one another, God dwelled in us, and his love is perfected in us. No man hath seen God at anytime, so how is it that the world has pictures who they say is God, and believes they are God, despite the scripture saying no man hath seen God at anytime? Revelation 12:9; And the great dragon was cast out, that old serpent, called the Devil, and Satan, which deceives the whole world: he was cast out into the earth, and his angels were cast out Introduction with him. Because the devil has deceived the whole world! If your pastor has a picture that is supposed to be Christ in the church, or home, or condones them in society as being Christ, he is a false prophet come out from among him and be you separate.

2 Corinthians 4:13; We having the same spirit of faith, according as it is written, I believed, and therefore have I spoken; we also believe, and therefore speak; We have the same spirit of faith, according as it is written, we believe, therefore we speak what's written, so if it's not written that Christ was white with blonde hair and blue eyes, then how do you have faith if what you believe is not written? You not even saved!

Humus Soil
So how did God create man and what did he look like? Genesis 2: 6 - But there went up a mist from the earth, and watered the whole face of the ground. When water gets on the ground, it makes the soil fertile in which when something is fertile, it is able to produce an offspring because it's capable of reproducing. For example, a woman can't just have a baby she has to be fertile first and she becomes fertile by first, ovulating which then she ripens and releases an egg or eggs from the ovary for possible fertilization. So God ripen and released water onto the ground to make it fertile to produce an offspring. So now that the ground, which is soil, is able to reproduce or give life, what did God do next?

Genesis 2:7; And the LORD God formed man of the dust of the ground, and breathed into his nostrils the breath of life; and man became a living soul. So from the soil of the ground, God formed man and breathed into his nostrils the breath of life, and man became a living soul. The garden of Egypt is located in Northern East Africa in which today its existence and location is known as the Fertile Crescent, because of its nutrients in the soil that makes it so fertile to give life to plants and other things. Humus is an organic component of soil which is mostly found in Northern East Africa. It is a dark brown organic component of soil that improves the water-retaining properties of soil, making it more fertile and workable. If color didn't matter, then it wouldn't have been described in the bible, and when John turned, he would have said I didn't see any color, I just see Christ, as to what should be said today's society. But the color of his skin is not what's going to save us Hebrews or the gentiles; it is by way of the Holy Spirit of God in receiving the gift of Salvation that is what saves us.

CHAPTER I

THE SPOKEN WORD

Hebrews 2:1-3

1We must pay the most careful attention, therefore, to what we have heard, so that we do not drift away. **2**For since the message spoken through angels was binding, and every violation and disobedience received its just punishment, **3**how shall we escape if we ignore so great a salvation? This salvation, which was first announced by the Lord, was confirmed to us by those who heard him.

John 1:1-8;14

The Word Became Flesh

1In the beginning was the Word, and the Word was with God, and the Word was God. **2**He was with God in the beginning. **3**Through him all things were made; without him nothing was made that has been made. **4**In him was life, and that life was the light of all mankind. **5**The light shines in the darkness, and the darkness has not overcome it.

6There was a man sent from God whose name was John. **7**He came as a witness to testify concerning that light, so that through him all might believe. **8**He himself was not the light; he came only as a witness to the light. **14**The Word became flesh and made his dwelling among us. We have seen his glory, the glory of the one and only Son, who came from the Father, full of grace and truth.

God Spoke Us Into Being. Everything exists by the Spoken Word of God. By His voice, He continually makes His will known to everything and everyone.

Throughout the first chapter of Genesis, God is set on bringing forth creation. He desires it, He speaks it, and it is. God said, "let there be light," and there was light. The sky, land, seas, vegetation, and living creatures were all created by a Spoken Word.

"Then God said, 'Let us make man in our image… so God created man…'" (Genesis 1:26-27).

It was thru God's words that gave us life. The spoken word written says God knew us before we were, and He spoke us into being.

"You saw me before I was born. Every day of my life was recorded in your book. Every moment was laid out before a single day had passed." Psalm 139:16

"Before I formed you in the (physical) womb I knew you, before you were born(physically) I set you apart..." Jeremiah 1:5

"For you created my inmost being; you knit me together in my mother's womb." Psalm 139:13

Thru his spoken word mankind was formed while still in the womb of the woman. He set in place every moment of every day of our lives before we ever took our first breath. He set us apart for His purpose before we took our first step – all because He spoke it into existence! God's voice, His Spoken Word, gives us physical life and establishes the purpose for our lives. How great are the plans God speaks over those who are His!

The Spoken Word - I AM…..YASHUA!!

The Ancient Of Days(old testament) Spoken Word of God in Jeremiah gives us a taste of His will for His people; He desires that we would be set apart and appointed for His service. The written word (new testament) reaffirms this:
"For this is the will of God, your sanctification." (1 Thessalonians 4:3)

So how does God's Spoken Word accomplish His will to sanctify us? Through His Son, which son Jesus of Nazareth the one they call the Messiah as stated: So when the crowd had gathered, Pilate asked them, "Which one do you want me to release to you: Jesus Barabbas, or Jesus who is called the Messiah?" Matt 27:16-17

"who is the real Jesus, that came to us from God, righteousness and sanctification and redemption." (1 Corinthians 1:30)....??

What is God's spoken words saying to us in these written Scriptures? We must be introduced to the Spoken Word of God; we must know the truth of Him. Is his name the Lord Jesus Christ they called the Messiah or Jesus Bar-Abbas which means in Aramaic "Son of my Father" or "Son of The Father".

CHRIST/MESSIAH

Christ is the Greek for "anointed one". The word "Messiah" is Hebrew with the same meaning. "In the beginning was the Word, and the Word was with God, and the Word was God" (John 1:1). Jesus Barabbas is the Word of God. The Bible, the written word, documenting and testifying to the Spoken Word of God, is not simply a book with words on pages; it is the manifestation life of the Ancient of Days(the old testament) and is revealed to us by the Spirit of God. "For the spoken word of God is alive and active." (Hebrews 4:12)

Jesus Bar-Abbas Son of The Father is the Word of God.

Jesus Bar-Abbas(Son of The Father) is the word of God 1 Peter The Word of God is Jesus Bar-Abbas. (Son of The Father)   He is alive, He embodies the fullness of God, and He reveals God's essence and character. Jesus Bar-Abbas (Son of The Father) is the Word of God not a murder or a thief. This is how we come to know the truth of God and how we know God, Himself – by listening to and trusting the Spoken Word of the Spirit of God within us, by walking in obedience to the Universal Prime Creator, through the Spirit of GOD within us, not looking outside of us. Those who look outside "Dreams", those who look inside is "Awaken"

"For you have been born again, not of perishable seed, but of imperishable, through the living and enduring word of God." (1 Peter 1:23)

"He replied, "Blessed rather are those who hear the word of God and obey it." (Luke 11:28)

"All written Scripture is God-breathed(spoken) and is useful for teaching, rebuking, correcting and training in righteousness, so that the servant of God may be thoroughly equipped for every good work." (2 Timothy 3:16-17)

By trusting in the (spoken) Word of God and following the example set by the Lord Jesus(bar-abbas), we are promised the ability to do everything that Christ(bar-abbas) did and more. "Very truly I tell you, whoever believes in me will do the works I have been doing, and they will do even greater things than these." (John 14:12).

Many children of God today never attain to this victorious life because, like the Israelites, when they hear His voice, they do not believe; as a result, their hearts are hardened. The word of God warns us to not walk in this way.

"Today when you hear his voice, don't harden your hearts as Israel did when they rebelled." (Hebrews 3:15)

Let us know today and let the Spirit within transform us! Thru universal laws and Spoken Word of God that reincarnate us from the dead heart and mind to the elevation of life. Empowering us to fulfill His promise… "and they will do even greater things than these."

"We must simplify and know that God has spoken."What does it mean to know God? First, we are commanded to do and speak His Word. "Let the one who has my word speak it faithfully." Jeremiah 23:28-29. To speak the word faithfully means to be in the know of the word fully. Our words, themselves, are powerless unless they are lived out. We must proclaim we know what we have in the power of God's spoken Word through our daily actions. "What good is it, my brothers and sisters, if someone claims to have faith but has no deeds? Can such faith save them? …faith by itself, if it is not accompanied by action, is dead." (James 2:14,17)

We must simply and sincerely believe that what God has spoken is true. Then we will begin to speak it and live it as truth. This is the know in action. This activates the power of the Spoken Word of God within us. So whether we need to reduce your own foolishness or encouragement in your daily life, it is found when we speak the Word over our hearts, our minds, and our circumstances and then walk it out. Speaking the Word of God over ourselves more simply means to completely know that what He says is true.

No matter the circumstance or how we may feel, the beauty of God's Spoken Word is that it is always true. When we know truth above our situation, we exalt our spiritual energy and vibrations, (which means transitioning from 3rd dimension up to the 5th dimension), as Lord of our lives. We hear it, think on it, practice it, and speak it.

When we know God in this way, we cannot help but to talk about it… because He works! He's real! He's the answer in every situation! And He's always victorious! And we come to know that God(The Universal Prime Creator)is greater than a faithful friend and beyond an earth father.

Truly, this is how we begin to have a genuine relationship with God. It is through the Spoken Word that we defy foolishness and maintain a true life. When we confront the fear, or deceptions in our lives with the Spoken Word of God, we activate greater power and authority which always lead to victory. We develop the way we think, speak, hear, and experience pure and perfect divine oneness with God. We are no longer "dead in our thinking" and circumstances. We no longer trust in our emotions, or past experiences in the world. We know the truth that brings life. Then as we make decisions from knowing Him, it is no longer we who do it, but the spirit who lives in us. This is where we find His power to say "no" to the foolishness of life and live in the freedom God intended for us.

So you also should consider yourselves to be dead to the power of sin and alive to God through Christ Jesus." (Romans 6:11)

What Will You Speak?
"The tongue has the power of life and death those who love it will eat of its fruit...." Proverbs 18:21

"God favors today the one through whom He can show His magnificence glory thru."The Spoken Word tells us that we have the power of life and death in what we say. The Spoken Word of God is the only lasting word that will make an impact for eternity. The only word of eternal hope and the only lasting legacy we can leave. Any other words will fall to the ground, but the Spoken Word of God will live forever.

 Jesus(Bar-Abbas) is the spoken word of God. Romans 10:8 tells us that the word of God "is near you; it is in your mouth and in your heart," that is, the word of faith we are proclaiming." (Romans 10:8)

For the one who truly seeks to live a righteous life in the know, the Spoken Word is within you, it lives in your heart and flows from your mouth.

Let us hear God's Spoken Word within. Let us dedicate ourselves in the know, to the powerful, transformed life for which we were set apart before the world began. May we speak God's Word with confidence and maturity, not wasting what we know, to an idle mind of this world!

"For every idle word men may speak, they will give account of it in the days of consequences thru breaking universal laws. For by your words you will be justified, and by your words you will be condemned." (Matthew 12:36-37).

In the written bible John the Baptist was asked, "Who are you?" his simple reply was "I am the voice of one calling in the wilderness, 'Make straight the way for the Lord." (John 1:23)

God favors today the one through whom He can show His magnificence glory. Will you hear His voice ? What will you say? May you be set apart this day for God. May His Spoken Word be activated in you, that you may bring forth the everlasting, transforming words of God.

The SPOKEN WORD produced the Written Word.

The Written Word we have is the Copy of the SPOKEN WORDS of JESUS(BAR-ABBAS Son Of The Father, Son Of GOD).

The WORDS we SPEAK now are the Outcome of BOTH.

So the WORD SPOKEN Produced the Words written, that can then be SPOKEN Once Again.

The POWER OF THE WORD of GOD is SPEAKING IT FORTH, DECREEING IT with your MOUTH.

So the Written Word can Never Replace the SPOKEN WORD, which is the SEED that Produces it to begin with.

In the Ancient Of Days(changed to the old testament by the Greek) God Spoke out to Abraham, in the know, he did not send him a written message

The Written Word is a COPY of the SPOKEN WORD, JESUS the WORD made Flesh.

We are Sons of Abraham, because he is the One who Received the SPOKEN WORD of the INCORRUPTIBLE SEED that Produced JESUS.

JESUS is the OUTCOME of the SPOKEN WORD ABRAHAM received from GOD.

We are the OUT COME of the SPOKEN WORD.

COMING TO OUR RIGHT MIND, putting away foolish ideas.

The PROBLEM we Encounter Concerning our WORDS, is the CARNAL MIND concept of what is written.

THE SPOKEN WORD
John 1:1 In the beginning is the Word, and the Word is with God, and the Word is God

God Spoke to Abraham/ (he did not send him a note to read) Abraham Acted on the Spoken Word of God, which Produced "THE KNOW"

God spoke to the Prophets. The prophets spoke to the Greek who wrote down what was SPOKEN TO THEM)

The Word God Spoke to Abraham became FLESH.

JESUS BAR-ABBAS became the Living Word.

The New Testament(the written word) comes from the Spoken Word (there were no bibles 2,000 years ago).

The Spoken Word

The Gospel was Spoken by Words to others, who then took those Words in the know and continued to carry them to others. That is how the Gospel was Preached.

The Incorruptible Seed was Gods original Spoken Word of Promise.

The written Epistles even TELL US TO SPEAK THE WORD

Matt 4:4
But he answered and said, It is written, Man shall not live by bread alone, but by every word that proceed out of the mouth of God.

John 6:63 It is the spirit that quicken; the flesh profit nothing: the words that I speak to you, they are spirit, and they are life.

The BREAD of LIFE is you Continuing to Speak GODS WORDS over your own Life. You are to SPEAK WORDS of LIFE and your Words will become Words of Life to others who need to hear the KNOW.

 The New Testament(the written word) the GOSPEL was PREACHED, (they did not read the gospel)

In the written man-u-script(man-u-write), it is said by JESUS to PREACH, or PROCLAIM that GOSPEL

Mark 16:15 and he said unto them, Go into all the world and preach the gospel to every creature

There was no BIBLE JESUS BAR-ABBAS(Son of The Father) issued this DECREE from.

Reading the Gospel is not Preaching the Gospel, you must SPEAK WORDS so that it will bring greater knowledge.

FAITH comes from HEARING the SPOKEN WORD of GOD.

When you Speak, your Words are SPIRITS, that impact the LIFE of others. You are to Speak the TRUTH in the know.

THE SPOKEN WORD/ THE BREAD OF LIFE

The written Epistles   TELL US TO SPEAK THE WORD/ CONFESS the WORD.

GOD is the First Word, and the Last Word/ He is the SPOKEN WORD. His Words are Spiritual energy, so his Words Produce Life

We are the SONS OF GOD(the Els), so we Hear only what the Father is Speaking. We Repeat what we Hear the Father saying.

Then Our Spoken Words is Spirit, and Life.

Proverbs 18:21
The tongue has the power of life and death, and those who love it will eat of its fruit.

THE writers of the New Testament TAUGHT by the SPOKEN WORD. They where Preachers, meaning they taught by Speech, Speaking out the Good News.
The written Word has become the letter of the Law, it is NOT PRODUCING anything SUPERNATURAL. People are using it just like they did the LAW, and don't understand it.

The Written Word did not become FLESH. It was the SPOKEN WORD that became FLESH.

And the Word was made flesh, and dwelt among us, (and we beheld his glory, the glory as of the only begotten of the Father,) full of grace and truth.

THE WORD SPOKEN TO ABRHAM MANIFESTED into Reality and took on FLESH.

JESUS BAR-ABBAS (Son Of The Father) is the outcome of Gods SPOKEN WORD of FAITH Spoken to Abraham

Matthew 5:2 And he opened his mouth and taught them.

Romans 10:8
But what does it say? "The word is near you, in your mouth and in your heart" (that is, the word of the know that we proclaim)

ONLY SPOKEN WORDS of FAITH are Seeds that are Sown into Hearts of the mind that will Hear.

PREACHING the GOSPEL, is Spreading or Scattering WORDS of FAITH that others receive and Continue to Sow and keep on Sowing .

2 Cor 3:3
Forasmuch as you are manifestly declared to be the epistle of Christ ministered by us, written not with ink, but with the Spirit of the living God; not in tables of stone, but in fleshy tables of the heart.

Gods Epistle is not written anywhere but on our HEARTS/ BY THE SPIRIT. The Word Epistle is something Written/ so Paul is saying that we are made Manifest of Christ, by what the Spirit is writing on our Hearts (not in letters of stone).

Each Generation of the INCORRUPTIBLE SEED is More Supernatural. The Incorruptible Seed Produces something MORE SUPERNATURAL as it EVOLES. And it will keeps on Evolving on into eternity.

CHAPTER II

The Image of GOD

FIRST WORK Gen. 1:24-25

"And God said, Let the earth bring forth the LIVING CREATURE AFTER HIS KIND, cattle, and creeping thing, and beast of the earth AFTER HIS KIND; and it was so. And God made (created) the beast of the earth AFTER HIS KIND, and cattle AFTER THEIR KIND, and everything that creeps upon the earth AFTER HIS KIND; and God saw that it was good." These land animals were doubtless the same kind as we have today. The fact that they were created, "AFTER THEIR KIND" which is 5 times repeated, shows that they were not evolved from one common species. That all the different species of animals were created "separately" is proven from the fact that when species are crossed their offspring are sterile. The crossing of the jackass and a mare is the mule, and a mule is a hybrid and is sterile. If the "Evolutionary Theory" of the development of animal and vegetable life was true, we should expect to find evidence to that effect in fossil remains of the intermediate links, and we should also see "evolutionary processes" at work now whereby higher orders of animal and plant life are coming into being. But we see nothing of the kind. Animal and plant life exists today in the same form that it had excited in the knowledge of man. The birds build their nests and raise their young as they always did. The beaver builds his dam, and the bee constructs his honeycomb as they have always done. Man alone, has the faculty of improving his mode of construction. This is seen in the development of farming instruments from the crude plow a winnowing fan to the complex plow and cultivator and the combined reaper, binder, and thresher. But here we can trace the steps by the obsolete specimens of farming implements. This is not true in the animal and vegetable kingdoms, for there we find no intermediary links. If the Evolutionary Theory is correct, it should apply, to man as well as animals, and we should see by the crossing of the best specimens of the human race the evolution of a SUPERMAN but the history of the race disproves this.

SECOND WORK Gen. 1:26-28

"And God said; Let US make man in OUR IMAGE, after OUR LIKENESS: and let them have dominion over the fish of the sea, and over the fowl of the air, and over the cattle, and over all the earth, and over every creeping thing that crept upon the earth. So God CREATED (Bara) man in His OWN IMAGE, in the IMAGE OF GOD CREATED (Bara) He him; male and female created He them. And God blessed them, and God said unto them, Be fruitful, and multiply, and REPLENISH THE EARTH, and subdue it; and have dominion over the fish of the sea, and over the fowl of the air, and over every living thing that moved upon the earth."

That man also was "CREATED" (Bara) shows that he has not descended from an ape. Man was made in the "IMAGE OF GOD not in the image of an "Ape," and was not formed from a brute, of the "Dust of the Earth." There is an "Impassable Gulf" between the lowest order of man and the highest type of beast that science has failed to bridge. The "Missing Link" has never been found. That the whole human race is of "One specie" and had a common origin (Acts 17:26) is clear from the fact that, when races of the earth's inhabitants marry, their offspring are not sterile but fertile. This nullifies the argument that the white races are of different origin, and that the white race alone is the Adamic race.

There is no contradiction between the first and second of Genesis as to the creation of man. The first chapter (Gen. 1:26-28) gives the FACT of his creation, the second, the MANNER OF IT. Gen. 2:7. One is supplementary to the other. In chapter one God is spoken of as "ELOHIM," the Creator; in chapter two, He is called "JEHOVAH" (The Lord) because He there enters into covenant relations with man.

At first the name "Jehovah" is joined with "Elohim" to remove all doubt as to the identity of the Being designated by the compound word. Now while either of these names would suit some passages, in others one would be more suitable than the other.

This accounts for the discriminating use of these two names by the sacred writers, and is an answer to those critics who claim that the Scriptures are a clumsy compilation of incongruous and diverse documents which they call Elohistic and Jehovistic. In Gen. 2:7 we are told that– "The LORD God formed (Yatsar, fashioned) man of the dust of the ground and breathed into his nostrils the 'Breath of Life; ' and man became a living soul." This may mean that the Lord God, fashioned man out of the "dust of the ground" as a sculptor fashions the statue out of clay, and then breathed into the earthy form the "Breath of Life." However it was done we know the work was threefold:

1. The formation of the "BODY" "And the Lord God formed man of the dust of the ground." 2. The gift of the "SPIRIT"-"And breathed into his nostrils the 'Breath of Life'." By this is not meant the "Holy Spirit," but the "Spirit" of the "natural man"-that part of man that must be indwelt by the Holy Spirit before he can. be born again. It is the "God Conscious" nature of man.

3. The SOULISH part of man-"And man became a 'Living Soul'." This is the seat of the "Self-Conscious" nature, of memory, the affections, etc. The two principal parts of man are the BODY and the SPIRIT, but as the functions of these are separate, one being physical and the other spiritual, a third part had to be supplied called the SOUL, intermediate between them, and through which they may communicate. Thus man became a- "Threefold Being." 1Thes. 5:23.

"The Threefold Nature of Man." In Adam, as originally created, the Soul was such a perfect medium of communication between the Body and the Spirit that there was no conflict between them. The three blended together in one harmonious whole. When man fell the soul became the "battlefield" of the Body and the Spirit, and the conflict began that Paul so graphically describes in Rom. 7:7-9.

Eve was not fashioned in the same way as Adam. She was made" sometime later. Adam had not found among all the creatures God had made a suitable companion, and God saw that it was not good for him to be alone, so He proceeded to make him a "helpmeet." To this end "The Lord God caused a 'deep sleep' to fall upon Adam and he slept; and He took one of his 'RIBS, ' and closed up the flesh instead thereof; and the 'RIB, ' which the Lord God had taken from man, made (builded) He a WOMAN, and brought her unto the man. And Adam said This is now bone of my bones, and flesh of my flesh; she shall be called WOMAN, because she was taken OUT OF MAN." Gen. 2:21-23. While Adam and Eve were not both fashioned in the same way they were not evolved from some lower creature, but were direct creations of God, "male and female created He them." Gen. 1:27. The reason why Eve was not fashioned separately from Adam, but was taken out of Adam's side, was to show that in their relation to each other as man and wife they were to be ONE FLESH. That's their interests and sympathies, etc., were to be one, and physically they were to be counterparts of each 'Other. Adam and Eve in their physical relation to each other are a type of Christ and the Church. When Eve was presented to Adam he said-"This is now bone of my bones, and flesh of my flesh;" and the Apostle Paul in speaking of the Church says "'we are members of His BODY, and of His FLESH, and of His BONES. For this cause shall a man leave his father and mother, and shall be joined unto his wife, and they two shall be one flesh. This is a great 'mystery; ' but I speak concerning Christ and the Church." Eph. 5:30-32.
Adam was not created a baby or a primitive savage, but a full-grown man perfect in intellect and knowledge, else he could not have named the beasts of the field and the fowls of the air. And the fact that his descendants had such skill in the invention of musical instruments and mechanical devices and could build cities and towers and such a vessel as the Ark, proves that the men of Antediluvian times were men of gigantic intellect and attainments, and that instead of man having "evolved upward" he has "degenerated downward." We see from Gen. 1:29-30, that animals and man were originally given only vegetable food, and that it was not until after the Fall that animals became carnivorous. And it was not until after the Flood that man was permitted to eat "flesh."

"Every moving thing that lives (animals) shall be meat for you; even as the green herb (.which had been their food) have I given you all things. But 'flesh' with the life thereof, which is the BLOOD THEREOF, shall ye not eat." Gen. 9:3-4. That is, that in eating "flesh" they must first drain the "blood" from it, because the "blood" is the LIFE of the animal. It was not until after the Exodus, when the Law was given from Mt. Sinai that God's chosen people the Jews were restricted as to the kind of creeping things, flying fowl, and beasts they should eat. Lev. 11:1-3. Note that all that God created was GOOD. "And God saw everything that He had made, and, behold it was VERY GOOD. And the evening and the morning were the Sixth Day." Gen. 1:31. God is not the author of evil. Evil is the fruit of sin and disobedience. Thorns, thistles, poisonous vines, weeds, noxious beasts, as the serpent, are all the results of sin. Thus the heaven and the earth were restored and repopulated during the six days or periods of the "Restoration Week." The Bible and Science are in exact accord as to the order of the 8 works of the Restoration Week. The following Diagram shows how these 8 works could be arranged in a different order 40, 320 times (1x 2x 3x 4x 5x 6x 7x 8 = 40, 320) without any two lines being alike. Surely Moses must have been inspired, for there was only ONE chance in 40, 320, that he would have recorded them in the order that science claims they occurred. This is one of the proofs of the Divine Inspiration of the Holy Scriptures. SEVENTH DAY Gen. 2:2-3. "And on the 'Seventh Day' God ended His work which He had made; and He RESTED on the Seventh Day from all His work which He had made. And God blessed the 'Seventh Day, ' and SANCTIFIED IT; because that in it He had RESTED FROM ALL HIS WORK which God created and made." By God here is meant God in His Triune capacity, for, as has been well said, God the FATHER created the matter, God the SON took the matter and made the worlds and all that exists upon them, and then God the HOLY SPIRIT breathed the "Breath of Life" into the things that have life. John 1:1-3. Eph. 3:9. Col. 1:12-14. God rested because His work was finished. That is the only justifiable reason for resting. God rested because His work was not only finished but was GOOD. There could be no reflection upon it. But when God's perfect work was marred by sin, by the "Fall of Man," His "Sabbath Rest" was broken.

As soon as man fell it was necessary for God to resume His work, this time not to continue the creation of material things, but for the purpose of the redemption of man that he might become a "NEW CREATION" in Christ Jesus. 2Cor. 5:17. So Jesus in explaining His mission said– "My Father worked hitherto (in creation) and I work (now in REDEMPTION)." John 5:17. "BUT" and there is a "BUT".

The Creative Order was not about the first man and the first woman named Adam and Eve. They were not first man & woman on earth. The "ELs"(sons of God) were life on earth billions of light years before them. The creative order was simply about the existence of "Man & Woman" on earth, "Being Centered in Oneness" known as the "Creation Of Love". So let's start here with the biblical storyline of what the serpent said to the woman, " surely You are not going to die. But God knows at as soon as you eat of it, your eyes will be truly opened, and you will be like divine spirits who know good and evil. When the woman saw that the tree was good for eating and a delight to the eyes, and that the tree was desirable as a source of wisdom, she took of its fruit and ate. She also gave some to her husband and he ate. 1) Evaluate this verse on its own. What does it say about the woman's character? 2) What does it say about how she feels about her husband? About the snake? About God? The man said, "The woman you put at my side she gave me of the tree, and I ate. And the Lord God said to the woman, "What is this that you have done!" And the woman replied, "The serpent duped me, and I ate." 1) Blaming and not taking responsibility of the garden. Now they are cursed and kicked out He has to work; she has to suffer childbirth. Marriage be saved. You Think? Let's explore things from a scholarship level of thinking if we will.

Let us bring in the term "Exegesis", which means a writer not understanding the original content and writing in accords to how one feels what something means. So with this being said that Adam & Eve bit into a piece of tangible fruit preferably an apple that cause them to fall in sin and knowing good and evil. So the real question is... Can you bite into any apple or any parts of a fruit today and become greatly knowledgeable of "Good & Evil"? I don't think so. The book of Genesis and the bible has so many contradictions for instants, Proverbs "18:21 says...The tongue has the power of life and death, and those who love it will eat of its fruit".

So what we have here is a manuscript dilemma where we all been taught by way of the bible society of Christianity that eve bit into a piece of fruit and both fell into sin. But in the storyline, the devil by way of the snake was the one constantly speaking to her in a questionable manner. This is the part where writers didn't understand the original content (etymology), it was the words flowing off the tongue of the snake that was the fruit manipulating Adam & Eve to accept all things, (feeding the thinking) NOT TANGIBLE FRUIT. There are other biblical contradictory accounts of humanity's creation, known as the Priesthood version that appears in Genesis 1:26-27. Here, God made the man and fashions the woman simultaneously when the text reads: "So God created mankind in the divine image, male and female God created them." In Genesis 2. This is the version of Creation that most people are familiar with. God creates Adam, then places him in the Garden of Eden. Not long afterwards, God decides to make a companion for Adam and creates the animals of the land and sky to see if any of them are suitable partners for the man. God brings each animal to Adam, who names it before ultimately deciding that it is not a "suitable helper." God then causes a deep sleep to fall upon Adam and while the man is sleeping God fashions the woman from his side. When Adam awakes he recognizes the woman as part of himself and accepts her as his companion. The second account of Creation is known as the Yahwistic(Yahweh creation), ancient priest noticed two contradictory versions of Creation appear in the book of Genesis (which is called Bereisheet in Hebrew). They solved the discrepancy in two ways:

•	The first version of Creation actually referred to Adam's first wife, a 'first Eve.' But Adam was displeased with her, so God replaced her with a 'second Eve' that met Adam's needs.

•	The Priestly account describes the creation of an androgyne – a creative creature that was both male and female (Genesis Rabbah 8:1, Leviticus Rabbah

•	14:1). This creature was then split into a man and a woman in the Yahwistic account.

Although the tradition of two wives – two Eves – appears early on, this interpretation of Creation's timeline was not associated with the character of Lilith until the medieval period. God's beautiful plan for woman bring order and fulfillment as it is followed in obedience. God's plan is that men and women, exist in equal standards before Him, but of different roles and should be centered in oneness. In His wisdom and grace He specifically created each for his or her role. At creation, God caused a deep sleep to fall on Adam, and from him God took a rib and made a woman. She was a direct gift from the hand of God, made from man and for man (1 Corinthians 11:9). "Male and female He created them", each different but made to complete and complement one another in all. Although the woman is considered the "weaker vessel" (1 Peter 3:7), this does not make her inferior. She was made with a purpose in life that only she could fill. The woman has been given one of the greatest privileges in the world today, that of molding and nurturing a living soul. Her influence, especially in that of motherhood, affects her children's eternal destination. Even though Eve brought condemnation upon the world with her act of disobedience, God considered women worthy of a part in the plan of redemption (Genesis 3:15). "But when the fullness of the time was come, God sent forth his Son, made of a woman." (Galatians 4:4). He entrusted to her to the bearing of and the caring for his own Son. The woman's role is not insignificant! A distinction that is taught throughout the scriptures. Paul teaches if a man has long hair, it is a shame to him, but if a woman has the same long hair, it is her glory(1 Corinthians 11:14, 15). "The woman shall not wear that which pertained to a man, neither shall a man put on a woman's garment: for all that do so are abominations to God" (Deuteronomy 22:5). Their roles are not to be interchangeable. In the Garden of Eden, God said, "It is not good that the man should be alone," and He made a help meet for him-a companion, someone to satisfy his needs. Proverbs 31...tells in detail what kind of help meet the woman should be. And that of a supportive role of the wife to the husband is very evident in this description of the ideal woman. She ..will do him good and not evil. Because of her honesty, modesty and chastity, "her husband do safely trust in her." By her efficiency and diligence she would look well to her household. The basis of her virtue is "a woman that feared the Lord." This is a reverential fear that gives meaning and purpose to her life. Only as a heart of being centered in oneness can the woman be what's meant to be.

To become a child of God she needs to accept being centered in oneness through awareness of self as a god or goddess in the Kingdom of GOD. When a man and woman is aware of how to operate from a higher level consciousness they will be able to live a self-denied life. The Comforter is the holistic nature of the woman and thru the woman comes strength, courage, and direction to fulfill the duties of life between the man and the woman. When a man is aware of his position as a god(John 10:34;Psalms 82:6...“I said, 'You are "gods"; you are all sons of the Most High.') He gives life with humility, modesty, and with that inner "ornament of a meek and quiet spirited energy, which is in the sight of God a great price" (1 Peter 3:3, 4). Proper, modest dress adds to the hidden charms of the woman. She should never draw such attention to her body by being overdressed or underdressed. To avoid confusion and establish order, someone needs to be the head and God has ordained this position to be the man. Marriage is to be a harmonious relationship similar to that of the universal nature of man and GOD. Man is subjected to GOD, and the woman is subjected to man. So for any woman to rebel at her position in the framework of authority she then rebels against GOD. As the wife reverences her husband, she is obedient to the creative order, as to the nature of the scriptures (Ephesians 5:33), and her husband is then greatly able to bear all the responsibility of being in a higher consciousness position known as "Being Centered in Oneness". The liberation movement has challenged the universal laws for the women of today's times and era. Women are clamoring for freedom and fulfillment by asking for total equality. This puts them into a power struggle into a competitive role instead of a complementary partnership or spiritual awakening of a love experience over tangible love. Their quest for freedom only leads the woman into physical and mental bondage. Nevertheless, the selfishness of mankind is without excuse. In this case many of the women's frustrations can be understood. Ironically, the very thing that many women are rejecting is God's way of establishing the woman in a love experience of life that fully satisfies their hunger for love. If women move aggressively into the man's world and there seeks independence, equality, she loses her femininity that is reserved, modest sweetness that men and God respects approve of. Fulfillment comes as she cultivates those gifts for which she was created.

A woman's submission to the love experience in a relationship with a man liberates her from a multitude of frustrating problems. Her submission to God's order frees her from guilt. Submission to the love experience is a blessing, not a curse! The pattern of men taking the masculine leadership role and women following along in a feminine mindset elevates the man & woman to being centered in oneness. A key component to the single women's transition to becoming a married women as well as one's daughters becoming a wife at some point and time. As submission to the pleasure of the "Love Experience" in the relationship constantly see growth, an outward sign of the woman's submission to the universal laws, are tangibly seen in recognizing her "God Man" as well. Under the Christians scriptural guidelines the woman is commanded to have her head covered for praying and prophesying (1 Corinthians 11:3-5). Man is subject to Christ and should therefore pray with his head uncovered. Woman is subject to man and should pray with her head covered. Wearing a head covering is recognition of this divine order. From an ancestral standpoint "Higher Level Consciousness" means being centered in oneness. In other words when a man reaches this point he become a god like being, the Love Experience(love without pursuing a sex goal)with his woman becomes her covering, his "Crown" in a relationship is "Being Centered in Oneness" which is pure. It is a given for pleasure as well as for life from the universal prime creator. The woman was uniquely created for the special tasks in being a guide to the right path, serenity, peace comfort, nurturing to the man and child bearing, a creative fulfillment. the scriptures stated, "Be fruitful and multiply" (Genesis 1:28). The woman's key task is the management or maintain her home. Many modern day women chooses career, hires a baby-sitter, and rushes her children through childhood so that she can be free to pursue her self-interests in life. The scriptures states that women are to be "keepers at home" (Titus 2:5), ancestral wisdom teaches that the wisdom of the woman is the architect of the home. In other words the woman built the home, where the love experience with her God man, teaching and enjoying life on earth as well as applying the homemaking arts with joy in her heart. The woman is the heartbeat of turning a house into a home to which she helps lay the foundation of moral standards. The warmth of her spirit become quiet established security in the lives of the children's confidence. That in spite of their problems and fears, all is well.

The larger question is, Why would any woman trade this noble place for some dollars earned from some coveted(having obsession)position that leads to pain? The Universal Prime Creator's is not old fashioned power and authority, but it's the universal creative order. The women who wholeheartedly accept the "Universal Creative Order" is greatly rewarded. In instances that gives an extension to a woman's role beyond her home. Examples are given thru out history of goddess mindset like women who had responsibilities in Ancient Kingdom Royal Empires before their demise by destructive colonialism. But today there is a place where religious rules and regulations dictate to the woman how to serve within the Church building instead of the primary place of worship called the home. As she express naturally born attributes of pleasures of the love experience, gentleness, compassion, comforting and nurturing ways, she is living a complex life. One of which becomes confusion and frustration for both her and the man. Older women are exhorted at all times to teach the young women the ways of how ancestral cultural works. Women, who do not have the cares of a home and a family, are able to fill a special place in the area of greater learning process. There are definite guidelines for women's behavior under a Matriarchal lesson of learning the home life. They are not at no time to usurp authority over the God man(those who walk as universal sons of GOD on earth). The Matriarch teaches, the order that God has planned for women, that they learn how to learn true service to being in a royal family called the Kingdom. Faithful women will find that place of higher level consciousness in the elevation, from the lower level consciousness which is security-ego, sensation-emotions, power-position. And seek to remain in greater level of service where they can humbly and consistently remain "Being Centered in Oneness". As the woman fill her role with the "Creation Of Love" of God in her heart, live in submissive obedience to the "Love Experience", and humbly give of herself in the daily practices of life. This leads to "Fulfill of the Man's Thirst and "Serve A Woman's Hunger". It fills the honorable place in God's plan that brings about a beautiful harmony of ETERNAL LIFE.

CHAPTER III

Who Is Constantine

The Great Constantine and Christianity

Constantine's vision and the Battle of the Milvian Bridge in a 9th-century Byzantine manuscript. During the reign of the Roman emperor Constantine the Great (306–337 AD), Christianity began to transition to the dominant religion of the Roman Empire. Historians remain uncertain about Constantine's reasons for favoring Christianity, and theologians and historians have often argued about which form of early Christianity he subscribed to. There is no consensus among scholars as to whether he adopted his mother Helena's Christianity in his youth, or, as claimed by Eusebius of Caesarea, encouraged her to convert to the faith he had adopted.

Constantine ruled the Roman Empire as sole emperor for much of his reign. Some scholars allege that his main objective was to gain unanimous approval and submission to his authority from all classes, and therefore he chose Christianity to conduct his political propaganda, believing that it was the most appropriate religion that could fit with the imperial cult. Regardless, under the Constantinian dynasty Christianity expanded throughout the empire, launching the era of the state church of the Roman Empire. Whether Constantine sincerely converted to Christianity or remained loyal to paganism is a matter of debate among historians. His formal conversion in 312 AD is almost universally acknowledged among historians despite that it was claimed he was baptized only on his deathbed by the Arian bishop Eusebius of Nicomedia in 337AD the real reasons behind it remain unknown and are debated also. According to a professor emeritus of history, Constantine's conversion was a matter of real politic, meant to serve his political interest in keeping the empire united under his control: The prevailing spirit of Constantine's government was one of conservatism. His conversion to and support of Christianity produced fewer innovations than one might have expected; indeed they served an entirely conservative end, the preservation and continuation of the Empire. Constantine's decision to cease the persecution of Christians in the Roman Empire was a turning point for early Christianity, sometimes referred to as the Triumph of the Church, the Peace of the Church or the Constantinian shift. In 313, Constantine and Licinius issued the Edict of Milan decriminalizing Christian worship.

The emperor became a great patron of the Church and set a precedent for the position of the Christian emperor within the Church and raised the notions of orthodoxy, Christendom, ecumenical councils, and the state church of the Roman Empire declared by edict in 380. He is revered as a saint and isapostolos in the Eastern Orthodox Church, Oriental Orthodox Church, and various Eastern Catholic Churches for his example as a Christian monarch.

Before Constantine

The first recorded official persecution of Christians on behalf of the Roman Empire was in AD 64, when, as reported by the Roman historian Tacitus, Emperor Nero attempted to blame Christians for the Great Fire of Rome. According to Church tradition, it was during the reign of Nero that Peter and Paul were martyred in Rome. However, modern historians debate whether the Roman government distinguished between Christians and Jews prior to Nerva's modification of the Fiscus Judaicus in 96 AD, from which point practicing Jews paid the tax and Christians did not.

Christians suffered from sporadic and localized persecutions over a period of two and a half centuries. Their refusal to participate in the imperial cult was considered an act of treason and was thus punishable by execution. The most widespread official persecution was carried out by Diocletian beginning in 303. During the Great Persecution, the emperor ordered Christian buildings and the homes of Christians torn down and their sacred books collected and burned. Christians were arrested, tortured, mutilated, burned, starved, and condemned to gladiatorial contests to amuse spectators. The Great Persecution officially ended in April 311AD, when Galerius, senior emperor of the Tetrarchy, issued an edict of toleration which granted Christians the right to practice their religion, although it did not restore any property to them.

Constantine, caesar in the Western Empire, and Licinius, caesar in the East, also were signatories to the edict. It has been speculated that Galerius' reversal of his long-standing policy of Christian persecution has been attributable to one or both of these caesars.

Conversion of Constantine's

It is possible that Constantine's mother, Helena, exposed him to Christianity. In any case, he only declared himself a Christian after issuing the Edict of Milan. Writing to Christians, Constantine made clear that he believed that he owed his successes to the protection of the High God alone.

Apollo the god

Jugate gold multiple issued by Constantine at Ticinum in 313AD, showing the emperor and the god Sol, with Sol also depicted in his quadriga on Constantine's shield. Follis issued by Constantine at Lugdunum 309–310AD, with Sol holding a globe and wearing a radiant crown. In 310AD a panegyric, preserved in the Panegyrici Latini collection and delivered at Trier for the joint occasion of the city's birthday and Constantine's quinquennalia, recounted a vision apparently seen by the emperor while journeying between Marseille and Trier. The panegyricist recounts that the god Apollo appeared to Constantine in company with Victoria and together presented him with three wreaths representing thirty years of power. This vision was perhaps in a dream experienced by the emperor while practising incubation at the shrine of Apollo Grannus in Grand, Vosges. Eusebius was aware of this vision, or reports of it, and refers in his own Panegyric of Constantine of 336AD to "tricennial crowns" bestowed by the hand of God in Christianity on Constantine, "augmenting the sway of his kingdom by long years".

Eusebius of Caesarea and other Christian sources record that Constantine experienced a dramatic series of events sometime between his father Constantius Chlorus's death in 306AD and the Battle of the Milvian Bridge on 28 October 312AD. The battle secured Constantine's claim to the title of augustus in the West, which he had assumed unilaterally when his father died. According to the Eusebius' Life of Constantine, Constantine saw a vision of "a cross-shaped trophy formed from light" above the sun at midday.

About the time of the midday sun, when the day was just turning, he said he saw with his own eyes up in the sky and resting over the sun, a cross-shaped trophy formed from light, and a text attached to it which said, "By this conquer." Amazement at the spectacle seized both him and the whole company of soldiers which was then accompanying him on a campaign he was conducting somewhere, and witnessed the miracle.

According to Eusebius, Constantine had a dream that night. In the dream, the Christ of God appeared to him with the sign which had appeared in the sky, and urged him to make himself a copy of the sign which had appeared in the sky, and to use this as a protection against the attacks of the enemy.

—Eusebius of Caesarea, writing his Church History shortly after 313AD, makes no mention of this story in that work and does not recount it until composing his posthumous biography of Constantine decades afterwards. Life of Constantine was written by Eusebius after Constantine had died, and Eusebius admitted that he had heard the story from Constantine long after it had happened. Lactantius, writing 313–315AD and around twenty years before Eusebius's Life, also does not mention a vision in the sky. Instead, Lactantius mentions only that Constantine's dream took place on the eve of the climactic battle on the Ponte Milvio across the Tiber, with the crucial detail that the "sign" was marked on the Constantinian soldiers' shields. According to Lactantius:

Constantine's dream in the 9th Century

Constantine was advised in a dream to mark the heavenly sign of God on the shields of his soldiers and then engage in battle. He did as he was commanded and by means of a letter X turned sideways, with the top of its head bent around (transversa X littera, summo capite circumflexo), he marked Christ on their shields (Christum in scutis notat). Armed with this sign, the army took up its weapons. It is unclear what Constantine saw and what was marked on his army's shields. Eusebius's description of the daytime vision suggests a cross-shaped (either T or †) symbol, whereas Lactantius's description suggests a staurogram (□), although the crux ansata(☥) or the Egyptian ankh (□) have been proposed as interpretations as well.

All of these symbols were used by Christians in the 3rd and 4th centuries. Eusebius concurs with Lactantius that a new device was added to Constantine's soldiers' shields but does not connect this with the Battle of the Milvian Bridge, saying only that the "sign of the saving trophy" was marked, but not specifying when. Sometime after 317AD, Eusebius was permitted by Constantine, probably either in 325AD or in 335AD, to see a standard that was made according to the emperor's dream of instructions during the civil war. He described it as:

A tall pole plated with gold had a transverse bar forming the shape of a cross. Up at the extreme top a wreath woven of precious stones and gold had been fastened. On it two letters, imitating by its first characters the name "Christ," formed the monogram of the Saviour's title, rho being intersected in the middle by chi ... From the transverse bar, which was bisected by the pole, hung suspended a cloth ... But the upright pole ... carried the golden head-and-shoulders portrait of the God beloved Emperor, and likewise of his sons.

The description of Eusebius's, written after 324AD, suggests a more elaborate symbol than does Lactantius's earlier text, involving the Greek letters rho (P) and chi (X) ligatured as the chi rho ($\mathrm{\chi\rho}$), a monogram of Ancient Greek: χριστός, romanized: khrīstós, lit. 'anointed', referring to Jesus. Possibly Eusebius's description refers to a chi-rho inside the loop of an ankh. Following the battle and the defeat and death of Maxentius, Constantine became the undisputed emperor in the West and performed an adventus, a ceremonial entrance to the city. Arriving inside Rome's walls he ignored the altars to the gods prepared on the Capitoline Hill and did not carry out the customary sacrifices to celebrate a general's victorious entry into Rome, instead heading directly to the imperial palace. This is probably because the traditional Roman triumph, concluding with the sacrifice to Jupiter Optimus Maximus at his temple on the Capitoline, was traditionally celebrated after victory over Rome's enemies, rather than after the conquest of the city by a claimant in a civil war. The Arch of Constantine, for which numerous reliefs from earlier monuments depicting prior emperors sacrificing to various gods were re-carved with the face of Constantine, does not have an image of Constantine sacrificing to Jupiter, although he is shown sacrificing to Apollo and to Hercules.

Edict of Milan

In 313AD Constantine and Licinius announced "that it was proper that the Christians and all others should have liberty to follow that mode of religion which to each of them appeared best," thereby granting tolerance to all religions, including Christianity. The Edict of Milan went a step further than the earlier Edict of Serdica by Galerius in 311AD, returning confiscated Church property. This edict made the empire officially neutral with regard to religious worship; it neither made the traditional religions illegal nor made Christianity the state religion, as occurred later with the Edict of Thessalonica of 380AD. The Edict of Milan did, however, raise the stock of Christianity within the empire and reaffirmed the importance of religious worship to the welfare of the state. Most influential people in the empire, especially high military officials, had not been converted to Christianity and participated in traditional Roman religion; Constantine's rule exhibited a willingness to appease these factions. Coins minted up to eight years after the battle still bore the images of Roman gods. The monuments he first commissioned, such as the Arch of Constantine, contained no reference to Christianity.The accession of Constantine was a turning point for early Christianity. After his victory, Constantine took over the role of patron of the Christian faith. He supported the Church financially, had a number of basilicas built, granted privileges (e.g., exemption from certain taxes) to clergy, promoted Christians to high-ranking offices, returned property confiscated during the Great Persecution of Diocletian, and endowed the church with land and other wealth. Between 324AD and 330AD, Constantine built a new city, New Rome, at Byzantium on the Bosporos, which was named Constantinople for him. Unlike "old" Rome, the city began to employ overtly Christian architecture, contained churches within the city walls, and had no pre-existing temples from other religions. In doing this, however, Constantine required those who had not converted to Christianity to pay for the new city. Christian chroniclers tell that it appeared necessary to Constantine "to teach his subjects to give up their rites and to accustom them to despise their temples and the images contained therein."

This led to the closure of temples because of a lack of support, their wealth flowing to the imperial treasure; Constantine did not need to use force to implement this. It was the chronicler Theophanes who added centuries later that temples "were annihilated", but this was considered "not true" by contemporary historians.

Constantine respected cultivated persons, and his court was composed of older, respected, and honored men. Men from leading Roman families who declined to convert to Christianity were denied positions of power yet still received appointments; even up to the end of his life, two-thirds of his top government were non-Christian.[citation needed] Constantine's laws enforced and reflected his Christian attitudes. Crucifixion was abolished for reasons of Christian piety but was replaced with hanging, to demonstrate the preservation of Roman supremacy. On March 7, 321, Sunday, which was sacred to Christians as the day of Christ's resurrection and to the Roman Sun God Sol Invictus, was declared an official day of rest. On that day markets were banned and public offices were closed, except for the purpose of freeing slaves. There were, however, no restrictions on performing farming work on Sundays, which was the work of the great majority of the population.

Some laws made during his reign were even humane in the modern sense and supported tolerance, possibly inspired by his Christianity: a prisoner was no longer to be kept in total darkness but must be given the outdoors and daylight; a condemned man was allowed to die in the arena, but he could not be branded on his "heavenly beautified" face, since God was supposed to have made man in his image, but only on the feet. Publicly displayed gladiatorial games were ordered to be eliminated in 325AD.
According to Eusebius, in 331AD Constantine had commissioned him to deliver fifty volumes of scriptures for the churches of Constantinople, which were to be bound in leather and easily portable. Only three or four churches are known certainly to have existed in Constantine's reign, but others appear to have been planned or established, for which the scriptures were commissioned. The volumes were likely gospel books containing the Canonical Gospels of the Four Evangelists rather than complete Bibles with the entire Biblical canon, which were very rare in antiquity.

Construction Of The Church

Athanasius (Apol. Const. 4) recorded around 340AD Alexandrian scribes preparing Bibles for Constans. Little else is known. It has been speculated that this may have provided motivation for canon lists, and that Codex Vaticanus and Codex Sinaiticus are examples of these Bibles. Together with the Peshitta and Codex Alexandrinus, these are the earliest extant Christian Bibles.

According to Socrates Scholasticus, Constantine commissioned the construction of the first Church of Hagia Irene in Constantinople, on the site occupied by the Justinian church of the same name. It commemorated the peace won by Constantine and Crispus's victory over Licinius and Licinius II at the Battle of Chrysopolis in 324AD; its name, the Church of the Holy Peace (Ancient Greek: Ἁγία Εἰρήνη, romanized: Hagía Eirḗnē, lit. 'Holy Peace') recalled the Altar of Peace (Latin: ara pacis) built by Augustus, the first deified Roman emperor. Two other large churches were dedicated to Saint Mocius and to Saint Acacius; both worthies had supposedly been martyred in Byzantium during the Diocletianic Persecution. The Church of St Mocius was supposed to have included parts of a former temple of Zeus or Hercules, though it is unlikely that such a temple existed on the site, which was without the walls of the Constantinian city as well as of erstwhile Severan Byzantium. According to Eusebius, Christian liturgies were also performed in Constantine's Mausoleum, the site of which became the Church of the Holy Apostles; although Eusebius does not mention any Byzantine church by name, he reports that Christian sites were numerous inside the city and around it. Later tradition ascribed to Constantine the foundations in Constantinople of the Church of Saint Menas, the Church of Saint Agathonicus, the Church of Saint Michael at nearby Anaplous, and the Church of Hagios Dynamis (Ancient Greek: Ἅγιος Δύναμις, romanized: Hagíos Dynamis, lit. 'Holy Power').

The Christian Emperorship
Enforcement Of Doctrine
The reign of Constantine established a precedent for the position of the Christian emperor in the Church.

Emperors considered themselves responsible to the gods for the spiritual health of their subjects, and after Constantine they had a duty to help the Church define and maintain orthodoxy. The Church generally regarded the definition of doctrine as the responsibility of the bishops; the emperor's role was to enforce doctrine, root out heresy, and uphold ecclesiastical unity. The emperor ensured that God was properly worshiped in his empire; what proper worship (orthodoxy) and doctrines and dogma consisted of was for the Church to determine.

Constantine had become a worshiper of the Christian God, but he found that there were many opinions on that worship and indeed on who and what that God was. In 316AD, Constantine was asked to adjudicate in a North African dispute of the Donatist sect (who began by refusing obedience to any bishops who had yielded in any way to persecution, later regarding all bishops but their own sect as utterly contaminated). More significantly, in 325AD he summoned the First Council of Nicaea, effectively the first ecumenical council (unless the Council of Jerusalem is so classified). The Council of Nicaea is the first major attempt by Christians to define orthodoxy for the whole state. Until Nicaea, all previous Church councils had been local or regional synods affecting only portions of the Church.

Nicaea dealt primarily with the Arian controversy. Constantine was torn between the Arian and Trinitarian camps. After the Nicene council and against its conclusions, he eventually recalled Arius from exile and then banished Athanasius of Alexandria to Trier.

Just before his death in May 337AD, it is claimed that Constantine was baptized into Christianity. Up until this time he had been a catechumen for most of his adult life. He believed that if he waited to get baptized on his death bed he was in less danger of polluting his soul with sin and not getting to heaven. He was baptized by his distant relative Arian Bishop Eusebius of Nicomedia or by Pope Sylvester I which is maintained by the Catholic Church, the Coptic Orthodox Church, the Antiochian Orthodox Church, the Greek Orthodox Church, the Russian Orthodox Church, the Serbian Orthodox Church, upon by many other Eastern Orthodox, Nestorian Orthodox, and Oriental Orthodox Churches.

During Eusebius of Nicomedia's time in the imperial court, the Eastern court and the major positions in the Eastern Church were held by Arians or Arian sympathizers. With the exception of a short period of eclipse, Eusebius enjoyed the complete confidence both of Constantine and Constantius II and was the tutor of Emperor Julian the Apostate. After Constantine's death, his son and successor Constantius II was an Arian, as was Emperor Valens.

Religious Suppression

Constantine's position on religions traditionally practiced in Rome evolved during his reign. In fact, his coinage and other official motifs, until 325AD, had affiliated him with the pagan cult of Sol Invictus. At first, Constantine encouraged the construction of new temples and tolerated traditional sacrifices; by the end of his reign, he had begun to order the pillaging and tearing down of Roman temples.

Beyond the limes, east of the Euphrates, the Sasanian rulers, perennially at war with Rome, had usually tolerated Christianity. Constantine is said to have written to Shapur II in 324AD and urged him to protect Christians under his rule. With the establishment of Catholicism as the state religion of the Roman Empire, Christians in Persia would be regarded as allies of Persia's ancient enemy. According to an anonymous Christian account, Shapur II wrote to his generals:
" You will arrest Simon, chief of the Christians. You will keep him until he signs this document and consents to collect for us a double tax and double tribute from the Christians for we Gods have all the trials of war and they have nothing but repose and pleasure. They inhabit our territory and agree with Caesar, our enemy. " Constantinian shift is a term used by some theologians and historians of antiquity to describe the political and theological aspects and outcomes of the 4th-century process of Constantine's integration of the imperial government with the Catholic Church that began with the First Council of Nicaea. The term was popularized by the Mennonite theologian John H. Yoder. The claim that there ever was a Constantinian shift has been disputed by a Peter Leithart argues that there was a "brief, ambiguous 'Constantinian moment' in the fourth century," but that there was "no permanent, epochal 'Constantinian shift'."

On 15 June the temple would be closed again, but for the vestal virgins and the Roman state would go about its normal affairs again. The survival of a religious faith depends on a continual renewal and affirmation of its beliefs, and sometimes on adapting its rituals to changes in social conditions and attitudes. To the Romans, the observance of religious rites was a public duty rather than a private impulse. Their beliefs were founded on a variety of unconnected and often inconsistent mythological traditions, many of them derived from the Greek rather than Italian models. Since Roman religion was not founded on some core belief which ruled out other religions, foreign religions found it relatively easy to establish themselves in the imperial capital itself. The first such foreign cult to make its way to Rome was the goddess Cybele around 204 BC. From Egypt the worship of Isis and Osiris came to Rome at the beginning of the first century BC Cults such as those of Cybele or Isis and Bacchus were known as the 'mysteries', having secret rituals which were only known to those initiated into the faith. During the reign of Julius Caesar Jews were granted freedom of worship in the city of Rome, in recognition of the Jewish forces which had helped him at Alexandria. Also very well known is the cult of the Persian sun god Mythras which reached Rome during the first century AD and found great following among the army. Traditional Roman religion was further undermined by the growing influence of Greek philosophy, particularly Stoicism, which suggested the idea of there being a single god. The beginnings of Christianity are very blurry, as far as historical fact is concerned. The birth date of Jesus himself is uncertain. (The idea of Jesus birth being the year 1 AD is due rather to a judgment made some 500 years after the event took place.) Many point to the year 4 BC as the most likely date for Christ's birth, and yet that remains very uncertain. The year of his death is also not clearly established. It is assumed it took place between AD 26 and AD 36 (most likely though between AD 30 and AD 36), during the reign of Pontius Pilate as prefect of Judaea. Historically speaking, Jesus of Nazareth was a charismatic Jewish leader, exorcist and religious teacher. To the Christians however he is the Messiah, the human personification of God. Evidence of Jesus' life and effect in Palestine is very patchy. He was clearly not one of the militant Jewish zealots, and yet eventually the Roman rulers did perceive him as a security risk.

Roman power appointed the priests who were in charge of the religious sites of Palestine. And Jesus openly denounced these priests, so much is known. This indirect threat to Roman power, together with the Roman perception that Jesus was claiming to be the 'King of the Jews', was the reason for his condemnation. The Roman apparatus saw itself merely dealing with a minor problem which otherwise might have grown into a greater threat to their authority. So in essence, the reason for Jesus' crucifixion was politically motivated. However, his death was hardly noticed by Roman historians. Jesus' death should have dealt a fatal blow to the memory of his teachings, were it not have been for the determination of his followers. The most effective of these followers in spreading the new religious teachings was Paul of Tarsus, generally known as Saint Paul. St Paul, who held Roman citizenship, is famed for his missionary voyages which took him from Palestine into the empire (Syria, Turkey, Greece and Italy) to spread his new religion to the non-Jews (for until then Christianity was generally understood to be a Jewish sect). Though the actual definite outlines of the new religion of that day is largely unknown naturally, the general Christian ideals will have been preached, but few scriptures can possibly have been available. The Roman authorities hesitated for a long time over how to deal with this new cult. They largely appreciated this new religion as subversive and potentially dangerous for Christianity with its insistence on only one god, seemed to threaten the principle of religious toleration which had guaranteed (religious) peace for so long among the people of the empire. Most of all Christianity clashed with the official state religion of the empire, for Christians refused to perform Caesar worship. This, in the Roman mindset, demonstrated their disloyalty to their rulers. Persecution of the Christians began with Nero's bloody repression of AD 64. This was only a rash and sporadic repression though it is perhaps the one which remains the most infamous of them all. The first real recognition Christianity other than Nero's slaughter was an inquiry by Emperor Domitian who supposedly, upon hearing that the Christians refused to perform Caesar worship, sent investigators to Galilee to inquire on his family, about fifty years after the crucifixion. They found some poor smallholders, including the great-nephew of Jesus, interrogated them and then released them without charge.

The fact however that the Roman emperor should take interest in this sect proves that by this time the Christians no longer merely represented an obscure little sect. Towards the end of the first century the Christians appeared to sever all their ties with the Judaism and established itself independently. Though with this separation form Judaism and Christianity emerged as a largely unknown religion to the Roman authorities and Roman ignorance of this new cult bred suspicion. Rumors were abounding about secretive Christian rituals; rumors of child sacrifice, incest and cannibalism. Major revolts of the Jews in Judaea in the early second century led to great resentment of the Jews and of the Christians, who were still largely understood by the Romans to be a Jewish sect. The repressions which followed for both Christians and Jews were severe. During the second century AD Christians were persecuted for their beliefs largely because these did not allow them to give the statutory reverence to the images of the gods and of the emperor. Also their act of worship transgressed the edict of Trajan, forbidding meetings of secret societies. To the government, it was civil disobedience. The Christians themselves meanwhile thought such edicts suppressed their freedom of worship. However, despite such differences, with Emperor Trajan a period of toleration appeared to set in. Pliny the Younger, as governor of Nithynia in 111 AD, was so exercised by the troubles with the Christians that he wrote to Trajan asking for guidance on how to deal with them. Trajan, displaying considerable wisdom, replied: ' The actions you have taken, my dear Pliny, in investigating the cases of those brought before you as Christians, are correct. It is impossible to lay down a general rule which can apply to particular cases. Do not go looking for Christians. If they are brought before you and the charge is proven, they must be punished, provided that if someone denies they are Christian and gives proof of it, by offering reverence to our gods, they shall be acquitted on the grounds of repentance even if they have previously incurred suspicion. Anonymous written accusations shall be disregarded as evidence. They set a bad example which is contrary to the spirit of our times. Christians were not actively sought out by a network of spies. Under his successor Hadrian which policy seemed to continue. Also the fact that Hadrian actively persecuted the Jews, but not the Christians shows that by that time the Romans were drawing a clear distinction between the two religions. The great persecutions of 165-180 AD under Marcus Aurelius included the terrible acts committed upon the Christians of Lyons in 177 AD.

This period, far more than Nero's earlier rage, was which defined the Christian understanding of martyrdom. Christianity is often portrayed as the religion of the poor and the slaves. This is not necessarily a true picture. From the beginning there appeared to have been wealthy and influential figures that at least sympathized with the Christians, even members of court. And it appeared that Christianity maintained its appeal to such highly connected persons. Marcia, the concubine of the emperor Commodus, for example used her influence to achieve the release of Christian prisoners from the mines. Had Christianity generally grown and established some routes across the empire in the years following the persecution by Marcus Aurelius, then it had especially prospered from about AD 260 onwards enjoying widespread toleration by the Roman authorities. But with the reign of Diocletian things would change. Towards the end of his long reign, Diocletian became ever more concerned about the high positions held by many Christians in Roman society and, particularly, the army. On a visit to the Oracle of Apollo at Didyma near Miletus, he was advised by the pagan oracle to halt the rise of the Christians. And so on 23 February 303 AD, on the Roman day of the gods of boundaries, the terminalia, Diocletian enacted what was to become perhaps the greatest persecution of Christians under Roman rule. Diocletian and, perhaps all the more viciously, his Caesar Galerius launched a serious purge against the sect which they saw as becoming far too powerful and hence, too dangerous. In Rome, Syria, Egypt and Asia Minor (Turkey) the Christians suffered most. However, in the west, beyond the immediate grasp of the two persecutors things were far less ferocious. The key moment in the establishment if Christianity as the predominant religion of the Roman empire, happened in 312 AD when emperor Constantine on the eve before battle against the rival emperor Maxentius had a vision of the sign of Christ (the so called chi-rho symbol) in a dream. And Constantine was to have the symbol inscribed on his helmet and ordered all his soldiers (or at least those of his bodyguard) to point it on their shields. It was after the crushing victory he inflicted on his opponent against overwhelming odds that Constantine declared he owed his victory to the god of the Christians. However, Constantine's claim to conversion is not without controversy. There are many who see in his conversion rather the political realization of the potential power of Christianity instead of any celestial vision.

Constantine had inherited a very tolerant attitude towards Christians from his father, but for the years of his rule previous to that fateful night in 312 AD there was no definite indication of any gradual conversion towards the Christian faith although he did already have Christian bishops in his royal entourage before 312 AD. But however truthful his conversion might have been, it should change the fate of Christianity for good. In meetings with his rival emperor Licinius Constantine secured religious tolerance towards Christians all over the empire. Until 324AD Constantine appeared to on purposely blur the distinction of which god it was he followed, the Christian god or pagan sun god Sol. Perhaps at this time he truly hadn't made up his mind yet. Perhaps it was just that he felt his power was not yet established enough to confront the pagan majority of the empire with a Christian ruler. However, substantial gestures were made toward the Christians very soon after the fateful Battle of the Milvian Bridge in 312 AD. Already in 313AD tax exemptions were granted to Christian clergy and money was granted to rebuild the major churches in Rome. Also in 314AD Constantine already engaged in a major meeting of bishops at Milan to deal with problems befalling the church in the 'Donatist schism'. But once Constantine had defeated his last rival emperor Licinius in 324 AD, the last of Constantine's restraint disappeared and a Christian emperor (or at least one who championed the Christian cause) ruled over the entire empire. He built a vast new basilica church on the Vatican hill, where reputedly St Peter had been martyred. Other great churches were built by Constantine, such as the great St John Lateran in Rome or the reconstruction of the great church of Nicomedia which had been destroyed by Diocletian. Apart from building great monuments to Christianity, Constantine now also became openly hostile toward the pagans. Even pagan sacrifice itself was forbidden. Pagan temples (except those of the previous official Roman state cult) had their treasures confiscated. These treasures were largely given to the Christian churches instead. Some cults which were deemed sexually immoral by Christian standards were forbidden and their temples were razed. Gruesomely brutal laws were introduced to enforce Christian sexual morality. Constantine was evidently not an emperor who had decided to gradually educate the people of his empire to this new religion. Far more the empire was shocked into a new religious order. But in the same year as Constantine achieved supremacy over the empire (and effectively over the Christian church) the Christian faith itself suffered a grave crisis.

Arianism, a heresy which challenged the church's view of God (The Father) and Jesus (the son) was creating a serious divide in the church. Constantine called the famous Council of Nicaea which decided the definition of the Christian deity as the Holy Trinity, God the father, God the son and God the Holy Spirit. Had Christianity previously been unclear about its message then the Council of Nicaea (together with council at Constantinople in 381AD) created a clearly defined core belief. However, the nature of its creation - a council - and the diplomatically sensitive way in defining the formula, to many suggests the creed of the Holy Trinity to be rather a political construct between theologians and politicians rather than anything achieved by divine inspiration. It is hence often sought that the Council of Nicaea represents the Christian church becoming a more worldly institution, moving away from its innocent beginnings in its ascent to power. The Christian church continued to grow and rise in importance under Constantine. Within his reign the cost of the church already became larger than the cost of the entire imperial civil service. As for emperor Constantine; he bowed out in the same fashion in which he had lived, leaving it still unclear to historians today, if he truly had completely converted to Christianity, or not. He was baptized on his deathbed. It was not an unusual practice for Christians of the day to leave their baptism for such a time. However, it still fails to answer completely to what point this was due to conviction and not for political purposes, considering the succession of his sons. One of the primary problems of early Christianity was that of heresy. Heresy as generally defined as a departure from the traditional Christian beliefs; the creation of new ideas, rituals and forms of worship within the Christian church. This was especially dangerous to a faith in which for a long time the rules as to what was the proper Christian belief remained very vague and open to interpretation. The result of the definition of heresy was often bloody slaughter. Religious suppression against heretics became to any account just as brutal as some of the excesses of Roman emperors in suppressing the Christians. If Constantine's conversion of the empire had been harsh, it was irreversible. When in 361AD Julian ascended to the throne and officially renounced Christianity, he could do little to change the religious make-up of an empire in which Christianity by then dominated. Had under Constantine and his sons being a Christian almost been a pre-requisite for receiving any official position, then the entire working of the empire by now had been turned over to Christians.

It is unclear to what point the population had converted to Christianity (though the numbers will have been rising quickly), but it is clear that the institutions of empire must by the time Julian came to power have been dominated by Christians. Hence a reverse was impossible, unless a pagan emperor of the drive and ruthlessness of Constantine would have emerged. Julian the Apostate was no such man. Far more does history paint him as a gentle intellectual, who simply tolerated Christianity in spite of his disagreement with it. Christian teachers lost their jobs, as Julian argued that it made little sense for them to teach pagan texts of which they did not approve. Also some of the financial privileges which the church had enjoyed were now refused. But by no means could this have been seen as a renewal of Christian persecution. In fact in the east of the empire Christian mobs ran riot and vandalized the pagan temples which Julian had re-instated. Was Julian not a violent man of the likes of Constantine when, his response to Christian outrage were never felt as he already died in AD 363. If his reign had been a brief setback for Christianity, it had only provided further proof that Christianity was here to stay.

The Power of the Church

With the death of Julian the Apostate matters quickly returned to normal for the Christian church as it resumed its role as the religion of the power. In 380 AD emperor Theodosius took the final step and made Christianity the official religion of state. Severe punishments were introduced for who disagreed with the official version of Christianity. Furthermore, becoming a member of the clergy became a possible career for the educated classes, for the bishops were gaining ever more influence. At the great council of Constantinople a further decision was reached which placed the bishopric of Rome above that of Constantinople. This in effect confirmed the church's more political outlook, as until the prestige of the bishoprics had been ranked according to the church's apostolic history. And for that particular time preference for the bishop of Rome evidently appeared to be greater than for the bishop of Constantinople. In 390 AD alas a massacre in Thessalonica revealed the new order to the world. After a massacre of seven thousand people the emperor Theodosius was excommunicated and required to do penance for this crime.

This did not mean that now the church was the highest authority in the empire, but it proved that now the church felt sufficiently confident to challenge the emperor on matters of moral authority. At Constantine's death at Nicomedia in 337 AD, three sons and two of his nephews were destined by the late emperor to succeed him. Though two of those sons were absent from Nicomedia with the consent of the third, Constantius, the other members of the imperial family, except two young cousins were slaughtered by the soldiery. The empire was thereafter by agreement parted between the three sons: Constantine taking the west, Constans the centre and Constantius the east. The eldest of the three new emperors was twenty one; their two cousins, Gallus and Julian, the nephews of the great Constantine, were in 337 AD aged twelve and six respectively. From the outset Constantius was thoroughly occupied in coping with the activities of the Persian King Sapor II. Was Constantius engrossed in the quarrel with the Persian Sapor II over Armenia, and then the real seat of the struggle soon was in Mesopotamia, where the war raged for some years without any decisive result. Both sides called into action Arab horsemen, who raided and wrought havoc far and wide; nine pitched battles were fought, in which, by admission of roman historians, the advantage generally laid with the Persians. Constantius himself was twice present; but it is safe to assume that his officers, not he, were responsible for the military direction. Meanwhile Constantius' brothers, Constantine and Constans, were quarreling and then actually fighting over the possession of Illyria. The elder, Constantine, was slain in an ambush near Aquileia (340 AD), and the younger, Constans, was recognized throughout the western dominion. But Constans now conducted himself as an irresponsible tyrant. Loyalties soon waned and when Magnentius was acclaimed by the legions while the emperor was away hunting, Constans could only flee for his life, only to be overtaken and slain on the Spanish coast. If Magnentius in 350AD was recognized immediately in the prefectures of Gaul and Italy, then in Illyria another general Vetranio was set up as emperor. In the east Constantius still locked horns with Sapor II. Alas the King of Persia was called to see to other problems in the east of Persia, as news reached Constantius of the death of Constans and two new emperors being in place in the west. Both Sapor II and Constantius left Mesopotamia, leaving behind a devastated no-man's-land.

The two new emperors meanwhile made haste to come to terms and to proffer their equal amity to the surviving son of Constantine in the east. But for Constantius reconciliation with his brother's murderer Magnentius was impossible. Far more won over Vetranio as his ally and took to war against Magnentius, defeating him at the grueling Battle of Mursa in Pannonia where 50'000 of the best troops of the imperial armies were left dead. Though Magnentius himself was not dead, he sought to continue the war, but his troops gradually deserted him. By the time those who remained were ready to deliver him to the enemy, if only to spare themselves, he chose suicide. Had Constantius left his cousin Gallus in charge of ruling the east, it was only to learn that Gallus was an irresponsible tyrant and was already planning on treason. Gallus was summoned to Pannonia where he met with an executioner's sword in 354 AD. Except for Constantius himself, the only surviving male descendant of Constantine the Great was Julian, the younger brother of Gallus. Julian lived in Athens devoting himself to literary and philosophical studies. He had no practical experience of rule and sought none. Yet against his will Julian was raised by Constantius to Caesar with the souvereignty over transalpine Europe. The fact that the empire was too large to be managed without viceroys was once more proving itself; especially since the Persian King Sapor II, having dealt with his problems to the east of Persia, was now back at the Roman borders to renew his ambitions. The barbarians moreover were again swarming over the upper Danube. Constantius occupied himself with the barbarian problem while his lieutenants dealt with Sapor in Mesopotamia. Though the Persian army was vastly superior in numbers, it eventually exhausted itself in several vain attempts to conquer the stubbornly defended fortress city of Amidia. Alas their numbers depleted and, though the war went on, the great threat to the eastern empire was averted. Meanwhile the reluctant Julian was proving himself a valiant man of action in Gaul and on the Gallic frontier. A strong man was certainly needed in Gaul; for in the civil war Magnentius had called to his aid hosts of Franks and Alemanni, who promptly assumed the role not of auxiliaries but of conquerors. Despite his inexperience and his academic predilections, Julian proved himself equal to the emergency, winning battles against heavy odds with distinguished personal valor, and restoring law and order in the devastated districts.

Until the reputation he was winning aroused the jealousy of Constantius, whose own credit was being not at all enhanced by his operations in the east, neither as soldier nor as ruler. Jealousy rapidly developed into suspicion and probably into secret designs against the life of the younger man. Constantius ordered an immediate dispatch of the best of the legions of Julian to the Mesopotamian front. The legions responded by calling upon Julian to save the empire by assuming the purple of Augustus. For some time Julian held out loyally, but the soldiery would take no denial till he yielded, at last convinced that loyalty to the empire was above loyalty to the emperor though Julian professed to demand only his own recognition as Western Augustus Constantius naturally refused to look on his as anything but a rebel. When this was made clear to Julian and his legions there remained no alternative but civil war. And suddenly Julian with no more than three thousand men vanished into the forests and mountains of south Germany to reappear on the lower Danube. Constantius, returning from his inglorious campaign in the east, was taken ill in Cilicia, and died 361 AD. There was no civil war. Julian the Apostate crossed over to Asia, his title of Augustus undisputed, and never returned to Europe. Julian reigned for no more than two years. He bears the name 'Apostate' because he renounced the Christianity of his earlier years and proclaimed himself the champion of the ancient gods. Though, if Julian did refute Christianity, his method of suppressing the religion he discarded was not that of persecution in the ordinary sense. He went no further than to exclude Christian teaching and teachers from the schools. For the rest of his reign Julian remained occupied with the Persian war. A victorious campaign in which he penetrated beyond the Tigris ended in disaster. The army advancing under the direction of rashly trusted guides was lead into a trap. It was almost overwhelmed by the myriads of foes by which it found itself surrounded. Yet valour and skill broke every onslaught. But in the pursuit which followed the last repulse, Julian was wounded by a javelin and was carried back to camp, only to die. (363 AD). There was no surviving male descendant of the imperial house and Julian had named no successor. The army chose an old soldier, Jovian, who lived long enough to patch up a peace with Persia and withdraw. But six months after his accession Jovian died. Again the choice lay with the soldiery. In 364 AD a barbarian of Pannonian stock and common descent but proved capability was elected to be Rome's new master, Valentinian.

By his first act the new emperor recognized the practical necessity for partition. No one man could successfully hold in his own hands for long the responsibility for both east and west. Valentinian chose for himself his native west, and made his brother Valens Augustus of the east. This time the division was permanent, though the empire still remained nominally one. For twelve years Valentinian ruled the west with vigor and, apart from his savage mercilessness toward any opposition, with justice and moderation. Valentinian was rigid in his insistence on equal treatment for all religions; he held the Gallic frontiers with a strong hand against swarming Franks and Alemanni who he defeated in successful campaigns beyond the Rhine. It was on a campaign against the Quadi on the upper Danube that one of those outbursts of ungovernable rage which marred his character wrought his own undoing inducing an apoplexy that killed him. On Valentinian's death, his elder son Gratian was at once recognized as his successor. Gratian's mother had been discarded by Valentinian in favor of a wife who bore him another son, Valentinian II, whom Gratian immediately named as co-emperor. Had since Constantine Christian emperors always been able to accept several religions in being within their empire then Gratian were the first to be unable to tolerate this. Had over time privileges been bestowed upon the church then the privileges for the state religion had still remained. The latter were now being withdrawn. In consequence none-Christians were beginning to grow restive, whilst the Christian church became increasingly intolerant of others. Meanwhile in the east still ruled Valens His appointment as emperor of the east proved to be the gravest error of judgment Valentinian had ever made. The worst faults of Valens were feebleness and indecision, not brutality. And to these weaknesses it was due that King Sapor II in his old age finally was able to establish complete if detested mastery over Armenia. However, the great disaster in the reign of Valens did not befall the empire till after the death of Valentinian. About the middle of the century the widespread Gothic confederation had been extending and consolidating its territories between the Baltic in the north and the Danube and Black Sea in the south, under the leadership of Hermanaric the Amal, whom all tribes recognized as King. But during the same period a new and formidable foe was pouring from Asiatic Scythia into European Scythia, the flood of the terrible Huns. Now it rolled down on the Goths.

Officially at the least the Goths were now friends of Rome. Reeling under the shock, the Visigoths sought the aid of Valens, who granted them wide lands for settlement on the southern side of the Danube barrier. Their vast swarms, only in part disarmed, were ferried across the river by hundreds of thousands, in numbers which had been utterly underestimated. The cramped starvation conditions to which they were subjected were wholly intolerable. Hence arose on the hither side of the Danube defenses a new enemy. Valens had in effect created his own disaster. War now raged in the Balkans, a war so critical that Valens called upon Gratian to come to his aid. But Gratian had hardly less serious embarrassment of his own, for the Alemanni were upon him. It was not until he had won a decisive crushing victory over them that he could report himself as on the march to affect a junction with the army in the east. But Valens would not wait. In the neighborhood of Adrianople he flung himself upon the Goths and in the battle that followed his army was annihilated, he himself perished, and the triumph of the Goths was complete (9 August 378 AD). The battle of Adrianoble stopped the advance of Gratian. Tremendous though the disaster had been, Adrianople and the greater capital on the Bosporus could defy the onslaughts of the Goths, who were no experts in siege warfare. But for Gratian to have marched on the Goths would have meant to risk disaster in both east and west. The Alemanni had been disposed of only for the moment. Gratian made haste to pronounce a new emperor in the east to take in hand the Gothic problem. His choice fell upon Theodosius, the son of a great captain and servant of the state on whom in Gratian's first year the intrigues of traitors had brought the undeserved penalty of treason. The son, who had already had time to prove his capacity, had been suffered to retire into private life; and was now raised to the purple at the age of thirty-three. Theodosius took up his hard task with admirable skill and prudence, but no lack of courage. Hermanaric had fallen before the Gothic war began. The able successor who had led the united Goths to victory died, and with his death their unity departed. Theodosius made no ambitious attempt to retrieve the position by staking the fate of the empire on a pitched battle. He risked no great engagements; but while he struck minor blows against their divided forces he encouraged their internal divisions.

His diplomacy attached some of their leaders to the empire, for which they had an almost superstitious reverence. In little more than four years a comparatively enduring if precarious peace was established. Gratian meanwhile was losing the high reputation he had won. Of his courage and his private virtues there could be no question, but the appearance of high capacity may have been due to his early submission to wise direction. Further he made the mistake of abandoning much of the cares of state for amusements, which brought him into contempt with the soldiery.

Theodosius had hardly set the seal on his own reputation in AD 382 by his much applauded treaty with the Goths, when the army in Britain, as in the days of Carausius, renounced its allegiance to Gratian and proclaimed an emperor of its own choice. The Spaniard Maximus reluctantly accepted the dangerous honor. In AD 383 Maximus crossed the Channel with a great force which depleted the garrison of the island, and marched upon Lutetia (Paris) where Gratian was residing. The soldiery in Gaul refused to move. Gratian fled, but was overtaken at Lyons, where he was treacherously assassinated, though without any connivance of the British emperor. The successful usurper had nothing to fear from the boy Valentinian II - or rather from his mother Justina - reigning at Milan. But he hastened to send an embassy to Theodosius, repudiating and condemning the murder which had been so hastily committed in his name, but justifying his own assumption of the purple and inviting the friendly alliance of the eastern emperor. Theodosius may well have felt that the pacification he had just effected was too precarious to warrant him in plunging the empire into a civil war, whose result would be doubtful, though justice and honor demanded the punishment of Gratian's murderer. He contented himself with recognizing the title of Maximus in the Gauls and Britain as a third Augustus, provided that the sovereignty of Valentinian II in Italy, Africa and western Ilyria were unquestioned. And to those terms Maximus agreed. But the excessive ambition of Maximus brought about his own downfall. Justina was unpopular as Italy was fanatically Christian orthodox, whereas she was an Arian heretic. Maximus seized this as an excuse to invade Italy. Justina fled to Theodosius with Valentinian II and her daughter.

The emperor fell in love with the daughter and married her. Theodosius' cautious policy was blown to the winds, Maximus was promptly wiped out and Valentinian II was restored to the empire of the west, where on his mother's death, he fell completely under the influence of the orthodox part (388 AD). His reign was brief although he had barely emerged from boyhood. The supreme command in Gaul was conferred on the pagan Frank, Arbogast, an able captain who had stood loyal to Gratian and had taken service with Theodosius instead of Maximus. The Frank now gave way to aspirations of his own. After a quarrel with Arbogast, Valentinian II committed suicide or was murdered, and Arbogast set up in hi place his own puppet, Eugenius in 392 AD. In 394 AD Theodosius disposed of the usurper, and divided the succession in east and west between his own sons Arcadius (382-408AD) and Honorius (AD 384-423AD). The latter at once became western emperor on the death of Theodosius in AD 395 Arcadius succeeded him at Constantinople. The young heirs of the powerful Theodosius were feeble and incompetent. From the death of Theodosius to the disappearance of the western empire, mighty figures stalked across the stage, but they were not of Roman or Byzantine emperors but of barbarians: Vandal, Visigoth, Ostrogoth, Frank, or - most terrible of all - Hun. Theodosius had named as the guardian of his sons and chief of his armies of the west a soldier of proven ability and worth, the Vandal Stilicho, who discharged his office with more loyalty than Arbogast the Frank. Virtualy the rule of the west was in his hands. While he was engaged in crushing the dangerous independence of a Moorish prince and tyrant, Gildo, in Africa, the misrule of prefect Rufinus at Constantinople brought on a great rebellion of the Visigoths - that branch of the Gothic race which had settled in Moesia and Illlyria, the Ostrogoths remaining beyond the Danube - led by Alaric the Balt. The Goths overran Greece practically unchecked and wrought much destruction, till the appearance of Stilicho, his work in Africa accomplished, stayed their conquering career. Alaric was in danger of being enveloped, but escaped with great skill, and in fact frightened the court of Constantinople into buying him off by appointing him to the command in Illyria as an imperial officer. The Goth accepted the position, but as a stepping stone. Italy was the objective on which he had fixed his ambitions. There were miscellaneous and for the most part barbarian troops now at his disposal were ready to follow him. And in 403 AD Honorius and Italy were terrified by an apparently wholly unexpected invasion.

In AD 472 Ricimer resolved to depose Anthemius, having proclaimed Olybrius (husband of the elder daughter of Valentinian III) emperor in his place. So Gundobad returned to Burgundy and Leo proclaimed Julius Nepos emperor in AD 474.Though already the following year Julius Nepos was a fugitive from Rome, ejected by his 'master of the soldiers', Orestes, who made his own son, contemptuously known as Romulus 'Augustulus', emperor. At the same time Zeno, the successor to Leo, was a fugitive from Constantinople, ejected by Basiliscus. Both usurpers fell in AD 476. In the east Zeno was restored, but in the west the Germanic mercenary Odoacer seized power. Odoacer chose not to be Augustus himself, nor to serve another western Augustus, but to be the viceroy of one Roman emperor in Constantinople. The Western Roman Empire had ceased to be.

In 1676 A.D., The Europeans nations that arrived in New England (North America) described the Aboriginal-Americans (Moors) to be BLACK AS GYPSIES (E-GYPTIANS). 1763 A.D., On October 7, 1763, King George R., of Great Britain's, Treaty with the Indigenous People (Indians) regarding land acquisitions and demarcation lines in America. The FOUR Colonies distinct and separate governments are called Quebec, East Florida, West Florida and Grenada. 1774 A.D., On October 20, 1774, British-American subjects of the British Empire form the First United Stated of America perpetual Constitutions in the Thirteen Colonies called, "The Articles of Association"'" recognized Moors as Moors not Negroes or Black-A-Moors. It is historically noted that in 1775 A.D., The first President of the Untied States of America under the Articles of Confederation was John Hanson, alleged Moor, a Maryland Shanwnee Native American patriot who fought in the American Revolution. In 1787 A.D., Assisted by England, Scotland, Ireland, Netherlands, France, Germany, Finland and Sweden the United States of America ended their war with the Moors (Moroccan Empire) and signed the Treaty of Peace and Friendship with the Emperor Mohammed III (Moorish-Mason). The aforementioned treaty is the longest unbroken treaty in the history of the United States.

On December 1, 1789, The Ninth President of the United States George Washington apologizes to his Masonic Brother Emperor Mohammed III, for not sending the regular advices (tribute: a payment by one ruler or nation to another as acknowledgment of submission or price of protection, excessive tax). Also, President Washington asked the Emperor to recognize their newly formed government. The Moroccan Empire (Moors) was the first nation to recognize the thirteen colonies as a sovereign nation. Allegedly the Emperor agreed to their recognition because 25 Moors were members of the first Continental Congress. The Continental Congress and the Moroccan-American Treaty of Friendship Turbulence ruled the early years of the United States of America. The new country continued the fight for freedom against the powerful British Empire. The central government of this new nation, the Continental Congress, negotiated through the limitations designed to keep the federal government from developing into a system with the same faults as the one they were seeking to   escape. However, at this time, our country's leaders included the very men schoolchildren learn about in their first American History classes. With figures like Benjamin Franklin, Thomas Jefferson, and John Adams involved in shaping the base for the country of the United States of America, the expectations and accomplishments are boundless for the country of Morocco, a similar success story, Sultan Sidi Muhammad Ben Abdullah, worked to develop a sound foundation for his country. Sultan Abdullah sought diplomatic and economic alliances to establish relationships with the naval powers and foreign traders influencing the Mediterranean Sea. Sultan Abdullah, finding the new American nation as an optimal partner for economic growth and political friendship, extended the olive branch to the new American diplomat, Benjamin Franklin. Completely unknown at the time, this offer of friendship would become the first contact for a relationship that lasts to this day. The Moroccan-American Treaty of Friendship overcame many obstacles initially, but today it is the longest standing foreign relations treaty for the United States of America. Before the development of the Morocco-American Treaty of Friendship, several key factors affected the process for formalizing the relationship and establishing a diplomatic and economic relationship between the two countries.

Having a large impact on the efforts to develop this treaty, was the continued involvement of the United States government in their fight for independence from the British Empire. Next, the French crown advised Benjamin Franklin to ignore the inquiries of the Moroccan Consul on this matter. These issues delayed the response of the United States, resulting in a strain between the two countries before establishing a relationship. Sultan Abdullah's first inquiry toward an economic treaty with the United States occurred in December of 1777 through a letter sent to Benjamin Franklin, at the time based in Paris as an American Diplomat to France. At the same time, the future of the United States as a country remained completely in doubt. Only a few months earlier, General Howe's troops forced the Continental Congress to flee Benjamin Franklin's home town of Philadelphia for York, Pennsylvania. In the same month as Sultan Abdullah's first inquiry, General Washington was establishing his winter base in Valley Forge. To compound the problems of establishing a relationship between the Moroccan and American governments, concerns arose about Etienne D'Audibert Caille, the consul appointed by Morocco to establish a relationship with the United States. As the Moroccan Consul in this matter, Caille initialized contact through a letter to Benjamin Franklin in Paris. Franklin initially ignored this communication based on advice from the French officials, "it was not safe to have any correspondence with him." Caille continued his efforts to establish a relationship with the United States by sending a second letter to Franklin in February of 1778; eventually Caille attempted another route to the United States government, the American diplomat in Madrid, John Jay. After a lack of response based on the letter to Jay, Caille eventually sent a letter directly to the Continental Congress of the United States Samuel Huntington, the president of the Continental Congress, acknowledged the receipt of Caille's letter. "I have lately received a Letter from an Officer, Consul under the Emperor of Morocco in Behalf of the Emperor inviting these United States to trade in his Ports, and giving Assurances that they may & shall enjoy all Privileges of any maritime Power, and that he is disposed to enter into a Treaty of Commerce with us." Huntington followed the United States Continental Congress's acknowledgement of Caille's letter with a response advising that the United States "receive with much Pleasure the Intimation of the generous and Princely Intentions of his Majesty the Emperor of Morocco".

However, this was not the end of the delays for the development of this relationship. It took nearly three years for the US to take the next step, when Benjamin Franklin, John Adams, and John Jay petitioned Congress to: "write in the name of the United States, to the Emperor of Morocco, a letter by which their characters and interest may be so materially affected; and to take such measures thereon, as may be proper and consistent with the interest of the said states." French officials, "it was not safe to have any correspondence with him." Caille continued his efforts to establish a relationship with the United States by sending a second letter to Franklin in February of 1778; eventually Caille attempted another route to the United States government, the American diplomat in Madrid, John Jay. After a lack of response based on the letter to Jay, Caille eventually sent a letter directly to the Continental Congress of the United States. Samuel Huntington, the president of the Continental Congress, acknowledged the receipt of Caille's letter."I have lately received a Letter from an Officer, Consul under the Emperor of Morocco in Behalf of the Emperor inviting these United States to trade in his Ports, and giving Assurances that they may & shall enjoy all Privileges of any maritime Power, and that he is disposed to enter into a Treaty of Commerce with us." Huntington followed the United States Continental Congress's acknowledgement of Caille's letter with a response advising that the United States "receive with much Pleasure the Intimation of the generous and Princely Intentions of his Majesty the Emperor of Morocco". However, this was not the end of the delays for the development of this relationship. It took nearly three years for the US to take the next step, when Benjamin Franklin, John Adams, and John Jay petitioned Congress to: "write in the name of the United States, to the Emperor of Morocco, a letter by which their characters and interest may be so materially affected; and to take such measures thereon, as may be proper and consistent with the interest of the said states." Even after these delays, the Congress fails to act on the petition by their European diplomats until May, 1784. Seven years after offering to establish a relationship with the new country, Sultan Abdullah's patience ended. Pirates working under the banner of the Moroccan government seized an American vessel in October of 1784.

This action caused the United States Continental Congress to a decision point: "The depredations of those pirates unless speedily put an end to by making a treaty with them, may prove very injurious to the Commerce of the United States, Congress have taken such steps as they think will accomplish this desirable end." Only months before this, unknown to Sultan Abdullah, the Continental Congress authorized Thomas Jefferson, Benjamin Franklin, and John Adams to frame a treaty between the United States and Morocco. The United States assigned Thomas Barclay to lead the negotiations with Morocco. Upon arriving in Marrakech, Morocco on June 19, 1786, Thomas Barclay and his Moroccan counterpart, Tahir Fannish, developed a treaty in a short time period. Sultan Abdullah sealed the treaty only four days after Barclay's arrival. The Treaty of Marrakech became official after the Continental Congress ratified it on July 18, 1787. This treaty, seven years in the making, took only four days to negotiate.

Twenty-five articles, broken down into three major areas: signal passing, port practices, and trade practices, comprise the Treaty of Marrakech. The area of signal passing involved the different expectations and activities that should be reviewed when ships of the two countries meet in open waters, including the responsibilities for defending a partner under attack and the salvage rights on partner country soil. Port practices covered the handling of partner vessels while in port. This outlined re-supply, handling and repair practices for both merchant and wartime vessels. The final area of the treaty covered the treaty practices between the two nations. This established the United States as 'most favored nation' status with Morocco, and outlined the rules and practices for merchants on both sides of the relationship. With the treaty established, the United States and Morocco began a relationship benefiting both countries, with the balance initially shifted toward the United States; however in recent years, the balance moved to the Moroccan side. Initially, the United States saw significance by providing a springboard for diplomatic relationships with other countries. Both countries used this as an economic growth opportunity for each country. After establishing the Moroccan-American Treaty of Friendship, or the Treaty of Marrakech, the relationship between the United States and Morocco has traveled through three different phases. The first of these phases is the Initial Relationship phase beginning with the signing of the Treaty of Marrakech by Thomas Barclay on June 23, 1786 and continued until the Moroccan nation became a protectorate of France in 1912.

The second phase, the French Occupation phase, began in 1912 and ended in 1956. The third and current phase, the Post-Independence phase, began in 1956. The initial phase of the relationship started on a fast pace. Only days after the signing of the treaty by Barclay in 1786, the negotiators continued to work and developed a Ship Seals agreement to coincide with the Treaty of Friendship. Following the establishment of the United States Constitution, George Washington sent a letter apologizing for the delays in communication between the United States and Morocco before the Treaty establishment: "...It gives me pleasure to have this opportunity of assuring your majesty that I shall not cease to promote every measure that may conduce to the friendship and harmony which so happily subsist between your empire and these. Within our territories, there are no mines of either gold or of silver, and this young nation, just recovering from the waste and desolation of a long war, has not, as yet, had time to acquire riches by agriculture and commerce. But our soil is beautiful, and our people industrious and we have reason to flatter ourselves that we shall gradually become useful to our friends.... may the Almighty bless your Majesty with his constant guidance and protection..." However, the death of Sultan Abdullah in early 1790 jeopardized the future of the Treaty of Friendship until Sultan Moulay Suliman communicated with James Simpson, the American Consul at Gibraltar:"....we are at peace, tranquility and friendship with you in the same manner as you were with our father who is in glory .... the Americans, I find, are the Christian nation my father most esteemed ... I am the same with them as my father was and I trust they will be so with me ....With good relations thus reaffirmed." Shortly after this communication, James Simpson became the American consul to Morocco, and opened the American Consulate in Tangiers in 1797. 1790 A.D., On Wednesday, January 20, 1790, A petition was presented to the House of Representatives from the Sundry (numerous) Free Moors, Subjects to the Prince under the Emperor of Morocco in Alliance with the United States of America. The Sundry Free Moors Act states that all Free Moors may be tried under the same Laws as the Citizens of (South Carolina) and NOT under the Negro Act. 1836, President Andrew Jackson worked out an indefinite extension on the Moroccan-American Treaty of Friendship. The initial phase of the Moroccan-American Treaty of Friendship ended in after the Treaty of Fez in 1912 determined set Morocco as a protectorate of France.

Long before the development of this treaty, as early as the 1830s, the French began to show interest in the affairs of the country of Morocco. In 1857 A.D., The DRED SCOTT Case from the United States Supreme Court; holds that Africans [Moors] imported [captured in an undeclared war of enslavement]. Into this country [Territory of the United States and Several States] and SOLD as (perpetual) Slaves, were not included nor intended to be included under the word "Citizen" in the Constitution, whether emancipated or not, and remained without rights or privileges except such as those which the government might grant them. The reason why Moors/Africans cannot be U.S. Citizens because the Moroccan Empire has a business arrangement with the British Empire [European Corporate Contract Citizens Caucasian Men], The United States is a foreign European corporation conducting trade and commerce in foreign lands. Then in 1904, the United Kingdom officially recognized the French 'sphere of influence' over Morocco. This recognition cause controversy in Europe resulting in the Algeciras Conference of 1906, with the United States showed support for the Moroccans by reaffirming their open door policy, calling for maintenance of order and guarantees of religious and racial toleration in Morocco, and declaring the United States neutral on the questions of domination of Morocco. In 1912, Morocco officially became a protectorate of the French. During World War II, Morocco contributed considerably to the Allied cause. The United States landed troops in Morocco, with Roosevelt sending a message to the Sultan about the situation: "I have been highly pleased to learn of the admirable spirit of cooperation that is animating you and your people in their relationships ... with the forces of my country. Our victory over the Germans will, I know, inaugurate a period of peace and prosperity, during which the Moroccan and French people of North Africa will flourish and thrive in a manner which befits their glorious past." Sultan Mohammed V replied: "... once the cessation of hostilities had been ordered and the commanders of your troops affirmed that they did not come as conquerors but as liberators ... We declared to Major General George Patton that as long as our prestige, soul, religion and traditions were respected ... they could rest assured that they found in Morocco only friends and collaborators.

After the landing of the troops in Morocco, the Allied forces held the Anfa Conference in a Casablanca suburb and decided to pursue the unconditional surrender of the Axis powers. During this conference, President Roosevelt offered the Moroccan country increased economic and trade cooperation, plus American educational and business support, with a final offer to push for Moroccan independence after the conclusion of World War II. After the conclusion of World War II, it did take some time for Morocco to gain independence from France. At this time, the Moroccan and American governments reaffirmed the Moroccan-American Treaty of Friendship again, with the United States raising their level of representation from Diplomatic Agent to Ambassador. Cavendish W. Cannon took his post as the first American Ambassador to Morocco on October 6, 1956. Today, the United States and Morocco continue to maintain relations through open communications and meetings. The Moroccan-American Treaty of Friendship overcame many obstacles initially, but today it is the longest standing foreign relations treaty for the United States of America.

Sultan Sidi Muhammad Ben Abdullah's dedication to the cause allowed the slow moving United States to establish a relationship with a foreign nation. The simple extension of an offer for diplomatic and economic relations by the Morocco brought legitimacy to the new American nation, and the efforts of the United States of America worked toward Morocco gaining independence from the French after World War II. The Hidden History of the Moorish People with the United States of America is recorded on the back of a Federal Reserve Note. There are two seals on the back of the $1.00, Federal Reserve Note (U.S. Currency) on the left side is the Great Seal of the Egyptian Moorish Empire and on the right is the Seal of the United States. There are over THIRTY THREE (33) passwords on the $1.00 (Note). The INDIGENOUS SOVEREIGN PEOPLE (Moors) who were betrayed by some of the European Colonial State Citizens who enslaved the Moors and branded them nigger, negro, black, colored, afro, hispanic, west indian, etc., seeking to conceal the Moroccan-American Treaty of Friendship.

Moroccan-American Treaty of Friendship (Treaty of Marrakech)
Articles 40

1) We declare that both Parties have agreed that this Treaty consisting of twenty five Articles shall be inserted in this Book and delivered to the Honorable Thomas Barclay, the Agent of the United States now at our Court, with whose Approbation it has been made and who is duly authorized on their Part, to treat with us concerning all the Matters contained therein. 2) Either the Parties shall be at War with any nation whatever the other Party shall not take a Commission from the Enemy nor fight under their Colors. 3)

If either of the Parties shall be at War with any Nation whatever and take a Prize belonging to that Nation, and there shall be found on board Subjects or Effects belonging to either of the Parties, the Subjects shall be set at Liberty and the Effects returned to the Owners. And if any Goods belonging to any Nation, with whom either of the Parties shall be at War, shall be loaded on Vessels belonging to the other Party, they shall pass free and unmolested without any attempt being made to take or detain them. 4) A Signal or Pass shall be given to all Vessels belonging to both Parties, by which they are to be known when they meet at Sea, and if the Commander of a Ship of War of either Party shall have other Ships under his Convoy, the Declaration of the Commander shall alone be sufficient to exempt any of them from examination. 5) If either of the Parties shall be at War, and shall meet a Vessel at Sea, belonging to the other, it is agreed that if an examination is to be made, it shall be done by sending a Boat with two or three Men only, and if any Gun shall be Bred and injury done without Reason, the offending Party shall make good all damages. 6) If any Moor shall bring Citizens of the United States or their Effects to His Majesty, the Citizens shall immediately be set at Liberty and the Effects restored, and in like Manner, if any Moor not a Subject of these Dominions shall make Prize of any of the Citizens of America or their Effects and bring them into any of the Ports of His Majesty, they shall be immediately released, as they will then be considered as under His Majesty's Protection. 7) If any Vessel of either Party shall put into a Port of the other and have occasion for Provisions or other Supplies, they shall be furnished without any interruption or molestation.

8) If any Vessel of the United States shall meet with a Disaster at Sea and put into one of our Ports to repair, she shall be at Liberty to land and reload her cargo, without paying any Duty whatever. 9) If any Vessel of the United States shall be cast on Shore on any Part of our Coasts, she shall remain at the disposition of the Owners and no one shall attempt going near her without their Approbation, as she is then considered particularly under our Protection; and if any Vessel of the United States shall be forced to put into our Ports, by Stress of weather or otherwise, she shall not be compelled to land her Cargo, but shall remain in tranquility until the Commander shall think proper to proceed on his Voyage. 10) If any Vessel of either of the Parties shall have an engagement with a Vessel belonging to any of the Christian Powers within gunshot of the Forts of the other, the Vessel so engaged shall be defended and protected as much as possible until she is in safety; And if any American Vessel shall be cast on shore on the Coast of Wadnoon or any coast thereabout, the People belonging to her shall be protected, and assisted until by the help of God, they shall be sent to their Country. 11) If we shall be at War with any Christian Power and any of our Vessels sail from the Ports of the United States, no Vessel belonging to the enemy shall follow until twenty four hours after the Departure of our Vessels; and the same Regulation shall be observed towards the American Vessels sailing from our Ports.- be their enemies Moors or Christians. 12) If any Ship of War belonging to the United States shall put into any of our Ports, she shall not be examined on any   Pretence whatever, even though she should have fugitive Slaves on Board, nor shall the Governor or Commander of the Place compel them to be brought on Shore on any pretext, nor require any payment for them. 13) If a Ship of War of either Party shall put into a Port of the other and salute, it shall be returned from the Fort, with an equal Number of Guns, not with more or less. 14) The Commerce with the United States shall be on the same footing as is the Commerce with Spain or as that with the most favored Nation for the time being and their Citizens shall be respected and esteemed and have full Liberty to pass and repasts our Country and Sea Ports whenever they please without interruption. 15) Merchants of both Countries shall employ only such interpreters, & such other Persons to assist them in their Business, as they shall think proper.

No Commander of a Vessel shall transport his Cargo on board another Vessel, he shall not be detained in Port, longer than he may think proper, and all persons employed in loading or unloading Goods or in any other Labor whatever, shall be paid at the Customary rates, not more and not less. 16) In case of a War between the Parties, the Prisoners are not to be made Slaves, but to be exchanged one for another, Captain for Captain, Officer for Officer and one private Man for another; and if there shall prove a deficiency on either side, it shall be made up by the payment of one hundred Mexican Dollars for each Person wanting; And it is agreed that all Prisoners shall be exchanged in twelve Months from the Time of their being taken, and that this exchange may be effected by a Merchant or any other Person authorized by either of the Parties. 17) Merchants shall not be compelled to buy or Sell any kind of Goods but such as they shall think proper; and may buy and sell all sorts of Merchandise but such as are prohibited to the other Christian Nations. 18). All goods shall be weighed and examined before they are sent on board, and to avoid all detention of Vessels, no examination shall   afterwards be made, unless it shall first be proved, that contraband Goods have been sent on board, in which Case the Persons who took the contraband Goods on board shall be punished according to the Usage and Custom of the Country and no other Person whatever shall be injured, nor shall the Ship or Cargo incur any Penalty or damage whatever. 19) No vessel shall be detained in Port on any presence whatever, nor be obliged to take on board any Article without the consent of the Commander, who shall be at full Liberty to agree for the Freight of any Goods he takes on board. 20) If any of the Citizens of the United States, or any Persons under their Protection, shall have any disputes with each other, the Consul shall decide between the Parties and whenever the Consul shall require any Aid or Assistance from our Government to enforce his decisions it shall be immediately granted to him. 21) If a Citizen of the United States should kill or wound a Moor, or on the contrary if a Moor shall kill or wound a Citizen of the United States, the Law of the Country shall take place and equal Justice shall be rendered, the Consul assisting at the Tryal, and if any Delinquent shall make his escape, the Consul shall not be answerable for him in any manner whatever.

22) If an American Citizen shall die in our Country and no Will shall appear, the Consul shall take possession of his Effects, and if there shall be no Consul, the Effects shall be deposited in the hands of some Person worthy of Trust, until the Party shall appear who has a Right to demand them, but if the Heir to the Person deceased be present, the Property shall be delivered to him without interruption; and if a Will shall appear, the Property shall descend agreeable to that Will, as soon as the Consul shall declare the Validity thereof. 23) The Consuls of the United States of America shall reside in any Sea Port of our Dominions that they shall think proper; And they shall be respected and enjoy all the Privileges which the Consuls of any other Nation enjoy, and if any of the Citizens of the United States shall contract any Debts or engagements, the Consul shall not be in any Manner accountable for them, unless he shall have given a Promise in writing for the payment or fulfilling thereof, without which promise in Writing no Application to him for any redress shall be made. 24) If any differences shall arise by either Party infringing on any of the Articles of this Treaty, Peace and Harmony shall remain notwithstanding in the fullest force, until a friendly Application shall be made for an Arrangement, and until that Application shall be rejected, no appeal shall be made to Arms. And if a War shall break out between the Parties, Nine Months shall be granted to all the Subjects of both Parties, to dispose of their Effects and retire with their Property. And it is further declared that whatever indulgences in Trade or otherwise shall be granted to any of the Christian Powers, the Citizens of the United States shall be equally entitled to them. 25) This Treaty shall continue in full Force, with the help of God for Fifty Years.

CHAPTER IV

The Vicar Of Christ

Vicar of Christ (from Latin Vicarius Christi) is a term used in different ways and with different theological connotations throughout history. The original notion of a vicar is as an "earthly representative of Christ", but it is also used in the sense of "person acting as parish priest in place of a real person." The title is now used in Catholicism to refer to the bishops and more specifically, was historically used to refer to the Bishop of Rome (the pope). An early appearance of a similar concept of the Vicar of Christ is mentioned in the Epistle to the Magnesians of St. Ignatius, Bishop of Antioch (who was possibly a disciple of both John the Apostle and Saint Peter), written between the years AD 88 and 107, which states: "your bishop presides in the place of God". Although Ignatius did not explicitly use the term Vicar of Christ, he sets out the concept, with regard to local bishops. More recently, the Second Vatican Council's Dogmatic Constitution on the Church Lumen gentium noted that bishops are "vicars and ambassadors of Christ," and the Catechism of the Catholic Church notes that each bishop governs his diocese " Christ's vicar."

The first recorded use of the term "Vicar of Christ" is found in the epistles of Tertullian in the late 2nd and early 3rd centuries, referring to the Holy Spirit,[6] that is, as Christ is not physically performing miracles in the Church, Holy Spirit acts as his Vicar on his behalf, performing miracles and preventing the Church from error. Other roles Tertullian attributed to the Holy Spirit as Vicar were: the direction of discipline, the revelation of the Scriptures, the reformation of the intellect, and the advancement toward the better things.

The third use of the term Vicar of Christ appears in the 5th century, in a synod of bishops to refer to Pope Gelasius I. The theological connotations of the title got a pastoral sense, evoking the words of Christ to the Apostle Peter, regarded by the first Catholic Pope in John 21:16-17, "Feed my lambs.. Feed my sheep". Catholics interpret this as Christ making Peter his vicar and pastor with the responsibility to feed his flock (the Church) in his own place.

However, the use of the title to refer to the popes in the early Church was unstable, and several variants of the use of Vicar were used for the Pope, as "Vicar of Peter", indicating that they were the successors of St. Peter,

"Vicar of the Prince of the Apostles" or "Vicar of the Apostolic", among other variants. This title is used by the Roman Missal in their prayers for a dead pope and the oath of allegiance to St. Boniface to Pope Gregory II. Since 1200, Popes have consistently used this title. Insisting that he and he alone—had the right to remove bishops from office, Pope Innocent III appealed to the title of Vicar of Christ. Occasionally, Popes like Nicholas III used "Vicar of God" as an equivalent title. The 2012 edition of the Annuario Pontificio gives "Vicar of Jesus Christ" as the second official title of the Pope (the first being "Bishop of Rome"). The edition of the same book published on March 25, 2020, included the title of "Vicar of Christ" to the section "Historical titles" section, to indicate its bond with the history of the papacy. The pope (Latin: papa, from Ancient Greek: πάππας, romanized: páppas, lit. 'father') is the bishop of Rome and the visible head of the worldwide Catholic Church. He is also known as the supreme pontiff, Roman pontiff, or sovereign pontiff. From the eighth century until 1870, the pope was the sovereign or head of state of the Papal States, and since 1929 of the much smaller Vatican City state. The reigning pope is Francis, who was elected on 13 March 2013. From a Catholic viewpoint, the primacy of the bishop of Rome is largely derived from his role as the apostolic successor to Saint Peter, to whom primacy was conferred by Jesus, who gave Peter the Keys of Heaven and the powers of "binding and loosing", naming him as the "rock" upon which the Church would be built.

While his office is called the papacy, the jurisdiction of the Episcopal See is called the Holy See. It is the Holy See that is the sovereign entity under international law headquartered in the distinctively independent Vatican City, a city-state which forms a geographical enclave within the conurbation of Rome, established by the Lateran Treaty in 1929 between Fascist Italy and the Holy See to ensure its temporal and spiritual independence. The Holy See is recognized by its adherence at various levels to international organizations and by means of its diplomatic relations and political accords with many independent states. According to Catholic tradition, the apostolic see of Rome was founded by Saint Peter and Saint Paul in the first century. The papacy is one of the most enduring institutions in the world and has had a prominent part in human history.

In ancient times, the popes helped spread Christianity and intervened to find resolutions in various doctrinal disputes. In the Middle Ages, they played a role of secular importance in Western Europe, often acting as arbitrators between Christian monarchs. In addition to the expansion of Christian faith and doctrine, modern popes are involved in ecumenism and interfaith dialogue, charitable work, and the defense of human rights.

Over time, the papacy accrued broad secular and political influence, eventually rivaling those of territorial rulers. In recent centuries, the temporal authority of the papacy has declined and the office is now largely focused on religious matters. By contrast, papal claims of spiritual authority have been increasingly firmly expressed over time, culminating in 1870 with the proclamation of the dogma of papal infallibility for rare occasions when the pope speaks ex cathedra—literally "from the chair (of Saint Peter)" to issue a formal definition of faith or morals. The pope is considered one of the world's most powerful people due to the extensive diplomatic, cultural, and spiritual influence of his position on both 1.3 billion Catholics and those outside the Catholic faith, and because he heads the world's largest non-government provider of education and health care, with a vast network of charities. The word pope derives from Ancient Greek πάππας (páppas) 'father'. In the early centuries of Christianity, this title was applied, especially in the East, to all bishops and other senior clergy, and later became reserved in the West to the bishop of Rome during the reign of Pope Leo I (440–461AD), a reservation made official only in the 11th century. The earliest record of the use of the title of 'pope' was in regard to the by-then-deceased patriarch of Alexandria, Heraclas (232–248AD). The earliest recorded use of the title "pope" in English dates to the mid-10th century, when it was used in reference to the 7th century Roman Pope Vitalian in an Old English translation of Bede's Historia ecclesiastica gentis Anglorum.

The Church Position

The Catholic Church teaches that the pastoral office, the office of shepherding the Church, that was held by the apostles, as a group or "college" with Saint Peter as their head, is now held by their successors, the bishops, with the bishop of Rome (the pope) as their head.

Thus is derived another title by which the pope is known, that of "supreme pontiff". The Catholic Church teaches that Jesus personally appointed Peter as the visible head of the Church, and the Catholic Church's dogmatic constitution Lumen gentium makes a clear distinction between apostles and bishops, presenting the latter as the successors of the former, with the pope as successor of Peter, in that he is head of the bishops as Peter was head of the apostles. Some historians argue against the notion that Peter was the first bishop of Rome, noting that the episcopal see in Rome can be traced back no earlier than the 3rd century.

The writings of Irenaeus, a Church Father who wrote around 180 AD, reflect a belief that Peter "founded and organized" the Church at Rome. Moreover, Irenaeus was not the first to write of Peter's presence in the early Roman Church. The Church of Rome wrote in a letter to the Corinthians (which is traditionally attributed to Clement of Rome about the persecution of Christians in Rome as the "struggles in our time" and presented to the Corinthians its heroes, "first, the greatest and most just columns", the "good apostles" Peter and Paul. Ignatius of Antioch wrote shortly after Clement; in his letter from the city of Smyrna to the Romans, he said he would not command them as Peter and Paul did. Given this and other evidence, such as Emperor Constantine's erection of the "Old St. Peter's Basilica" on the location of St. Peter's tomb, as held and given to him by Rome's Christian community, many scholars agree that Peter was martyred in Rome under Nero, although some scholars argue that he may have been martyred in Palestine.

Although open to historical debate, first-century Christian communities may have had a group of presbyter-bishops functioning as guides of their local churches. Gradually, episcopal sees were established in metropolitan areas. Antioch may have developed such a structure before Rome. In Rome, there were over time at various junctures rival claimants to be the rightful bishop, though again Irenaeus stressed the validity of one line of bishops from the time of St. Peter up to his contemporary Pope Victor I and listed them. Some writers claim that the emergence of a single bishop in Rome probably did not occur until the middle of the 2nd century. In their view, Linus, Cletus and Clement were possibly prominent presbyter-bishops, but not necessarily monarchical bishops.

Documents of the 1st century and early second century indicate that the bishop of Rome had some kind of pre-eminence and prominence in the Church as a whole, as even a letter from the bishop, or patriarch, of Antioch acknowledged the bishop of Rome as "a first among equals", though the detail of what this meant is unclear. Sources suggest that at first, the terms episcopos and presbyter were used interchangeably, with the consensus among scholars being that by the turn of the 1st and 2nd centuries, local congregations were led by bishops and presbyters, whose duties of office overlapped or were indistinguishable from one another. Some who say that there was probably "no single 'monarchical' bishop in Rome before the middle of the 2nd century ... and likely later."

In the early Christian era, Rome and a few other cities had claims on the leadership of worldwide Church. James the Just, known as "the brother of the Lord", served as head of the Jerusalem church, which is still honored as the "Mother Church" in Orthodox tradition. Alexandria had been a center of Jewish learning and became a center of Christian learning. Rome had a large congregation early in the apostolic period whom Paul the Apostle addressed in his Epistle to the Romans, and according to tradition Paul was martyred there.

During the 1st century of the Church (30–130), the Roman capital became recognized as a Christian center of exceptional importance. The church there, at the end of the century, wrote an epistle to the Church in Corinth intervening in a major dispute, and apologizing for not having taken action earlier. There are a few other references of that time to recognition of the authoritative primacy of the Roman See outside of Rome. In the Ravenna Document of 13 October 2007, theologians chosen by the Catholic and the Eastern Orthodox Churches stated:

Both sides agree that this canonical taxis was recognized by all in the era of the undivided Church. Further, they agree that Rome, as the Church that "presides in love" according to the phrase of St. Ignatius of Antioch (To the Romans, Prologue), occupied the first place in the taxis, and that the bishop of Rome was therefore the protos among the patriarchs.

They disagree, however, on the interpretation of the historical evidence from this era regarding the prerogatives of the bishop of Rome as protos, a matter that was already understood in different ways in the first millennium.

—Ravenna Document, 41

In AD 195, Pope Victor I (was of moor origin and was the first African pope), in what is seen as an exercise of Roman authority over other churches, excommunicated the Quartodecimans for observing Easter on the 14th of Nisan, the date of the Jewish Passover, a tradition handed down by John the Evangelist (see Easter controversy). Celebration of Easter on a Sunday, as insisted on by the pope, is the system that has prevailed.

The Edict of Milan in 313AD granted freedom to all religions in the Roman Empire, beginning the Peace of the Church. In 325AD, the First Council of Nicaea condemned Arianism, declaring trinitarianism dogmatic, and in its sixth canon recognized the special role of the Sees(is the central governing body of the Catholic Church and the Vatican City State)of Rome, Alexandria, and Antioch. Great defenders of Trinitarian faith included the popes, especially Liberius, who was exiled to Berea by Constantius II for his Trinitarian faith, Damasus I, and several other bishops.

In 380, the Edict of Thessalonica declared Nicene Christianity to be the state religion of the empire, with the name "Catholic Christians" reserved for those who accepted that faith. While the civil power in the Eastern Roman Empire controlled the church, and the patriarch of Constantinople, the capital, wielded much power, in the Western Roman Empire, the bishops of Rome were able to consolidate the influence and power they already possessed. After the fall of the Western Roman Empire, barbarian tribes were converted to Arian Christianity or Nicene Christianity; Clovis I, king of the Franks, was the first important barbarian ruler to convert to the mainstream church rather than Arianism, allying himself with the papacy. Other tribes, such as the Visigoths, later abandoned Arianism in favor of the established church.

After the fall of the Western Roman Empire, the pope served as a source of authority and continuity. Pope Gregory I (540–604) administered the church with strict reform. From an ancient senatorial family, Gregory worked with the stern judgment and discipline typical of ancient Roman rule. Theologically, he represents the shift from the classical to the medieval outlook; his popular writings are full of dramatic miracles, potent relics, demons, angels, ghosts, and the approaching end of the world.

Gregory's successors were largely dominated by the exarch of Ravenna, the Byzantine emperor's representative in the Italian Peninsula. These humiliations, the weakening of the Byzantine Empire in the face of the Muslim conquests, and the inability of the emperor to protect the papal estates against the Lombards, made Pope Stephen II turn from Emperor Constantine V. He appealed to the Franks to protect his lands. Pepin the Short subdued the Lombards and donated Italian land to the papacy. When Pope Leo III crowned Charlemagne (800AD) as emperor, he established the precedent that, in Western Europe, no man would be emperor without being crowned by a pope.

The low point of the papacy was 867–1049AD. This period includes the Saeculum obscurum, the Crescentii era, and the Tusculan Papacy. The papacy came under the control of vying political factions. Popes were variously imprisoned, starved, killed, and deposed by force. The family of a certain papal official who made and unmade popes for fifty years. The official's great-grandson, Pope John XII, held orgies of debauchery in the Lateran Palace. Emperor Otto I had John accused in an ecclesiastical court, which deposed him and elected a layman as Pope Leo VIII. John mutilated the Imperial representatives in Rome and had himself reinstated as pope. Conflict between the Emperor and the papacy continued, and eventually dukes in league with the emperor were buying bishops and popes almost openly.

In 1049AD, Leo IX travelled to the major cities of Europe to deal with the church's moral problems firsthand, notably simony and clerical marriage and concubinage. With his long journey, he restored the prestige of the papacy in Northern Europe.

From the 7th century, it became common for European monarchies and nobility to found churches and perform investiture or deposition of clergy in their states and fiefdoms, their personal interests causing corruption among the clergy. This practice had become common because often the prelates and secular rulers were also participants in public life.

To combat this and other practices that had been seen as corrupting the Church between the years 900 and 1050AD, centres emerged promoting ecclesiastical reform, the most important being the Abbey of Cluny, which spread its ideals throughout Europe. This reform movement gained strength with the election of Pope Gregory VII in 1073AD, who adopted a series of measures in the movement known as the Gregorian Reform, in order to fight strongly against simony and the abuse of civil power and try to restore ecclesiastical discipline, including clerical celibacy.

This conflict between popes and secular autocratic rulers such as the Holy Roman Emperor Henry IV and King Henry I of England, known as the Investiture controversy, was only resolved in 1122AD, by the Concordat of Worms, in which Pope Callixtus II decreed that clerics were to be invested by clerical leaders, and temporal rulers by lay investiture. Soon after, Pope Alexander III began reforms that would lead to the establishment of canon law.

Since the beginning of the 7th century, Islamic conquests had succeeded in controlling much of the southern Mediterranean, and represented a threat to Christianity. In 1095, the Byzantine emperor, Alexios I Komnenos, asked for military aid from Pope Urban II in the ongoing Byzantine–Seljuq wars. Urban, at the council of Clermont, called the First Crusade to assist the Byzantine Empire to regain the old Christian territories, especially Jerusalem. With the East–West Schism, the Eastern Orthodox Church and the Catholic Church split definitively in 1054. This fracture was caused more by political events than by slight divergences of creed. Popes had galled the Byzantine emperors by siding with the king of the Franks, crowning a rival Roman emperor, appropriating the Exarchate of Ravenna, and driving into Greek Italy.

In the Middle Ages, popes struggled with monarchs over power. From 1309 to 1377AD, the pope resided not in Rome but in Avignon. The Avignon Papacy was notorious for greed and corruption. During this period, the pope was effectively an ally of the Kingdom of France, alienating France's enemies, such as the Kingdom of England.

The pope was understood to have the power to draw on the Treasury of Merit built up by the saints and by Christ, so that he could grant indulgences, reducing one's time in purgatory. The concept that a monetary fine or donation accompanied contrition, confession, and prayer eventually gave way to the common assumption that indulgences depended on a simple monetary contribution. The popes condemned misunderstandings and abuses, but were too pressed for income to exercise effective control over indulgences.

Popes also contended with the cardinals, who sometimes attempted to assert the authority of Catholic Ecumenical Councils over the pope's. Conciliarism holds that the supreme authority of the church lies with a General Council, not with the pope. Its foundations were laid early in the 13th century, and it culminated in the 15th century with Jean Gerson as its leading spokesman. The failure of Conciliarism to gain broad acceptance after the 15th century is taken as a factor in the Protestant Reformation.

Various Antipopes challenged papal authority, especially during the Western Schism (1378–1417AD). It came to a close when the Council of Constance, at the high point of Concilliarism, decided among the papal claimants. The Eastern Church continued to decline with the Eastern Roman (Byzantine) Empire, undercutting Constantinople's claim to equality with Rome. Twice an Eastern emperor tried to force the Eastern Church to reunify with the West. First in the Second Council of Lyon (1272–1274AD) and secondly in the Council of Florence (1431–1449AD). Papal claims of superiority were a sticking point in reunification, which failed in any event. In the 15th century, the Ottoman Empire captured Constantinople and ended the Byzantine Empire. As part of the Catholic Reformation, Pope Paul III (1534–1549AD) initiated the Council of Trent (1545–1563AD), which established the triumph of the papacy over those who sought to reconcile with Protestants or oppose papal claims.

Protestant Reformers criticized the papacy as corrupt and characterized the pope as the antichrist. Popes instituted a Catholic Reformation (1560–1648AD), which addressed the challenges of the Protestant Reformation and instituted internal reforms. Pope Paul III initiated the Council of Trent (1545–1563), whose definitions of doctrine and whose reforms sealed the triumph of the papacy over elements in the church that sought conciliation with Protestants and opposed papal claims.

Gradually forced to give up secular power to the increasingly assertive European nation states, the popes focused on spiritual issues. In 1870, the First Vatican Council proclaimed the dogma of papal infallibility for the most solemn occasions when the pope speaks ex cathedra when issuing a definition of faith or morals. Later the same year, Victor Emmanuel II of Italy seized Rome from the pope's control and substantially completed the unification of Italy.

In 1929, the Lateran Treaty between the Kingdom of Italy and the Holy See established Vatican City as an independent city-state, guaranteeing papal independence from secular rule.[9] In 1950, Pope Pius XII defined the Assumption of Mary as dogma, the only time a pope has spoken ex cathedra since papal infallibility was explicitly declared. The Primacy of St. Peter, the controversial doctrinal basis of the pope's authority, continues to divide the eastern and western churches and to separate Protestants from Rome.

History of papal primacy
Church Fathers

The writings of several Early Church fathers contain references to the authority and unique position held by the bishops of Rome, providing valuable insight into the recognition and significance of the papacy during the early Christian era. These sources attest to the acknowledgement of the bishop of Rome as an influential figure within the Church, with some emphasizing the importance of adherence to Rome's teachings and decisions. Such references served to establish the concept of papal primacy and have continued to inform Catholic theology and practice.

In his letters, Cyprian of Carthage (210 – 258 AD) recognized the bishop of Rome as the successor of St. Peter in his Letter 55 (251 AD), which is addressed to Pope Cornelius, and affirmed his unique authority in the early Christian Church.

Cornelius (the Bishop of Rome) was made bishop by the choice of God and of His Christ, by the favorable witness of almost all the clergy, by the votes of the people who were present, and by the assembly of ancient priests and good men. And he was made bishop when no one else had been made bishop before him when the position of Fabian, that is to say, the position of Peter and the office of the bishop's chair, was vacant. But the position once has been filled by the will of God and that appointment has been ratified by the consent of us all, if anyone wants to be made bishop after that, it has to be done outside the church; if a man does not uphold the unity of the Church's unity, it is not possible for him to have the Church's ordination.

Irenaeus of Lyons (130 – 202 AD), a prominent Christian theologian of the second century, provided a list of early popes in his work Against Heresies III. The list covers the period from Saint Peter to Pope Eleutherius who served from 174 to 189 AD.

The blessed apostles [Peter and Paul], then, having founded and built up the Church [in Rome], committed into the hands of Linus the office of the episcopate. Of this Linus, Paul makes mention in the Epistles to Timothy. To him succeeded Anacletus; and after him, in the third place from the apostles, Clement was allotted the bishopric. ... To this Clement there succeeded Eviristus. Alexander followed Evaristus; then, sixth from the apostles, Sixtus was appointed; after him, Telephorus, who was gloriously martyred; then Hyginus; after him, Pius; then after him, Anicetus. Soter having succeeded Anicetus, Eleutherius does now, in the twelfth place from the apostles, hold the inheritance of the episcopate. Ignatius of Antioch (died 108/140AD) wrote in his "Epistle to the Romans" that the church in Rome is "the church that presides over love"....the Church which is beloved and enlightened by the will of Him that wills all things which are according to the love of Jesus Christ our God, which also presides in the place of the region of the Romans, worthy of God, worthy of honor, worthy of the highest happiness, worthy of praise, worthy of obtaining her every desire, worthy of being deemed holy, and which presides over love, is named from Christ, and from the Father, which I also salute in the name of Jesus Christ, the Son of the Father: to those who are united, both according to the flesh and spirit, to every one of His commandments; Augustine of Hippo (354 – 430 AD), in his Letter 53, wrote a list of 38 popes from Saint Peter to Siricius. The order of this list differs from the lists of Irenaeus and the Annuario Pontificio. Augustine's list claims that Linus was succeeded by Clement and Clement was succeeded by Anacletus as in the list of Eusebius, while the other two lists switch the positions of Clement and Anacletus.

For if the lineal succession of bishops is to be taken into account, with how much more certainty and benefit to the Church do we reckon back till we reach Peter himself, to whom, as bearing in a figure the whole Church, the Lord said: Upon this rock will I build my Church, and the gates of hell shall not prevail against it! Matthew 16:18. The successor of Peter was Linus, and his successors in unbroken continuity were these:— Clement, Anacletus, Evaristus...Other early Christian mentions Eusebius (260/265 – 339AD) mentions Linus as Saint Peter's successor and Clement as the third bishop of Rome in his book Church History. As recorded by Eusebius, Clement worked with Saint Paul as his "co-laborer".

As to the rest of his followers, Paul testifies that Crescens was sent to Gaul; but Linus, whom he mentions in the Second Epistle to Timothy as his companion at Rome, was Peter's successor in the episcopate of the church there, as has already been shown. Clement also, who was appointed third bishop of the church at Rome, was, as Paul testifies, his co-laborer and fellow-soldier.

—Eusebius of Caesarea, Church History, Book III, Chapter 4:9-10
Tertullian (155–220AD) wrote in his work "The Prescription Against Heretics" about the authority of the church in Rome. In this work, Tertullian said that the Church in Rome has the authority of the Apostles because of its apostolic foundation. Since, moreover, you are close upon Italy, you have Rome, from which there comes even into our own hands the very authority (of apostles themselves). How happy is its church, on which apostles poured forth all their doctrine along with their blood! Where Peter endures a passion like his Lord's! Where Paul wins his crown in a death like John's where the Apostle John was first plunged, unhurt, into boiling oil, and thence remitted to his island-exile!

According to reports, Clement of Rome was ordained by Saint Peter as the bishop of Rome. For this is the manner in which the apostolic churches transmit their registers: as the church of Smyrna, which records that Polycarp was placed therein by John; as also the church of Rome, which makes Clement to have been ordained in like manner by Peter.

Optatus the bishop of Milevis in Numidia (today's Algeria) and a contemporary of the Donatist schism, presents a detailed analysis of the origins, beliefs, and practices of the Donatists, as well as the events and debates surrounding the schism, in his book The Schism of the Donatists (367 A.D). Optatus wrote about the position of the bishop of Rome in maintaining the unity of the Church. You cannot deny that you are aware that in the city of Rome the episcopal chair was given first to Peter; the chair in which Peter sat, the same who was head—that is why he is also called Cephas ['Rock']—of all the apostles; the one chair in which unity is maintained by all. The Catholic Church teaches that, within the Christian community, the bishops as a body have succeeded to the body of the apostles (apostolic succession) and the bishop of Rome has succeeded to Saint Peter. Scriptural texts proposed in support of Peter's special position in relation to the church include:

Matthew 16:
I tell you, you are Peter, and on this rock I will build my church, and the gates of hell shall not prevail against it. I will give you the keys of the kingdom of heaven, and whatever you bind on earth shall be bound in heaven, and whatever you loose on earth shall be loosed in heaven.

Luke 22:
Simon, Simon, behold, Satan demanded to have you, that he might sift you like wheat, but I have prayed for you that your faith may not fail. And when you have turned again, strengthen your brothers.

John 21:
Feed my sheep.
The symbolic keys in the Papal coats of arms are a reference to the phrase "the keys of the kingdom of heaven" in the first of these texts. Some Protestant writers have maintained that the "rock" that Jesus speaks of in this text is Jesus himself or the faith expressed by Peter.

This idea is undermined by the Biblical usage of "Cephas", which is the masculine form of "rock" in Aramaic, to describe Peter.The Encyclopædia Britannica comments that "the consensus of the great majority of scholars today is that the most obvious and traditional understanding should be construed, namely, that rock refers to the person of Peter".

New Eliakim

According to the Catholic Church, the pope is also the new Eliakim, a figure in the Old Testament of the Bible who directed the affairs of the royal court, managed the palace staff, and handled state affairs. Isaiah also describes him as having the key to the house of David, which symbolizes his authority and power. Both Matthew 16:18–19 and Isaiah 22:22 show similarities between Eliakim and Peter getting keys which symbolize power. Eliakim gets the power to close and open, while Peter gets the power to bind and loose. According to the Book of Isaiah, Eliakim receives the keys and power to close and open.

I will place the key of the House of David on his shoulder; what he opens, no one will shut, what he shut's, no one will open.

—Isaiah, 22:22
According to the book of Matthew, Peter also gets keys and power to bind and loose.

I will give you the keys of the kingdom of heaven, and whatever you bind on earth shall be bound in heaven, and whatever you loose on earth shall be loosed in heaven.

—Matthew, 16:19
In the Books of Isaiah 22:3 and Matthew 16:18, both Eliakim and Peter are compared to an object. Eliakim to a peg (a structure that is driven into a wall or other structure to provide support and stability) while Peter to a rock. And I will fasten him like a peg in a secure place, and he will become a throne of honor to his father's house.

—Isaiah, 22:23
In Matthew 16:18 Peter was compared to a rock.

And I tell you, you are Peter, and on this rock I will build my church, and the gates of hell shall not prevail against it. The pope was originally chosen by those senior clergymen resident in and near Rome. In 1059, the electorate was restricted to the cardinals of the Holy Roman Church, and the individual votes of all cardinal electors were made equal in 1179. The electors are now limited to those who have not reached 80 on the day before the death or resignation of a pope. The pope does not need to be a cardinal elector or indeed a cardinal; since the pope is the bishop of Rome, only those who can be ordained a bishop can be elected, which means that any male baptized Catholic is eligible. The last to be elected when not yet a bishop was Gregory XVI in 1831, the last to be elected when not even a priest was Leo X in 1513, and the last to be elected when not a cardinal was Urban VI in 1378. If someone who is not a bishop is elected, he must be given episcopal ordination before the election is announced to the people.

The Second Council of Lyon was convened on 7 May 1274, to regulate the election of the pope. This Council decreed that the cardinal electors must meet within ten days of the pope's death, and that they must remain in seclusion until a pope has been elected; this was prompted by the three-year sede vacante following the death of Clement IV in 1268. By the mid-16th century, the electoral process had evolved into its present form, allowing for variation in the time between the death of the pope and the meeting of the cardinal electors.

Traditionally, the vote was conducted by acclamation, by selection (by committee), or by plenary vote. Acclamation was the simplest procedure, consisting entirely of a voice vote.

The conclave in Konstanz where Pope Martin V was elected
Since 1878, the election of the pope has taken place in the Sistine Chapel, in a sequestered meeting called a "conclave" (so called because the cardinal electors are theoretically locked in, cum clave, with key, until they elect a new pope).

Three cardinals are chosen by lot to collect the votes of absent cardinal electors (by reason of illness), three are chosen by lot to count the votes, and three are chosen by lot to review the count of the votes. The ballots are distributed and each cardinal elector writes the name of his choice on it and pledges aloud that he is voting for "one whom under God I think ought to be elected" before folding and depositing his vote on a plate atop a large chalice placed on the altar. For the Papal conclave, 2005, a special urn was used for this purpose instead of a chalice and plate. The plate is then used to drop the ballot into the chalice, making it difficult for electors to insert multiple ballots. Before being read, the ballots are counted while still folded; if the number of ballots does not match the number of electors, the ballots are burned unopened and a new vote is held. Otherwise, each ballot is read aloud by the presiding Cardinal, who pierces the ballot with a needle and thread, stringing all the ballots together and tying the ends of the thread to ensure accuracy and honesty. Balloting continues until someone is elected by a two-thirds majority. (With the promulgation of Universi Dominici Gregis in 1996, a simple majority after a deadlock of twelve days was allowed, but this was revoked by Pope Benedict XVI by motu proprio in 2007.) One of the most prominent aspects of the papal election process is the means by which the results of a ballot are announced to the world. Once the ballots are counted and bound together, they are burned in a special stove erected in the Sistine Chapel, with the smoke escaping through a small chimney visible from Saint Peter's Square. The ballots from an unsuccessful vote are burned along with a chemical compound to create black smoke, or fumata nera. (Traditionally, wet straw was used to produce the black smoke, but this was not completely reliable. The chemical compound is more reliable than the straw.) When a vote is successful, the ballots are burned alone, sending white smoke (fumata bianca) through the chimney and announcing to the world the election of a new pope. Starting with the Papal conclave, 2005, church bells are also rung as a signal that a new pope has been chosen.
The dean of the College of Cardinals then asks two solemn questions of the man who has been elected. First he asks, "Do you freely accept your election as supreme pontiff?" If he replies with the word "Accepto", his reign begins at that instant. In practice, any cardinal who intends not to accept will explicitly state this before he receives a sufficient number of votes to become pope.

The dean asks next, "By what name shall you be called?" The new pope announces the regnal name he has chosen. If the dean himself is elected pope, the vice dean performs this task. The new pope is led to the Room of Tears, a dressing room where three sets of white papal vestments (immantatio) await in three sizes. Donning the appropriate vestments and reemerging into the Sistine Chapel, the new pope is given the "Fisherman's Ring" by the camerlengo of the Holy Roman Church. The pope assumes a place of honor as the rest of the cardinals wait in turn to offer their first "obedience" (adoratio) and to receive his blessing. The cardinal protodeacon announces from a balcony over St. Peter's Square the following proclamation: Annuntio vobis gaudium magnum! Habemus Papam! ("I announce to you a great joy! We have a pope!"). He announces the new pope's Christian name along with his newly chosen regnal name.

Until 1978, the pope's election was followed in a few days by the papal coronation, which started with a procession with great pomp and circumstance from the Sistine Chapel to St. Peter's Basilica, with the newly elected pope borne in the sedia gestatoria. After a solemn Papal Mass, the new pope was crowned with the triregnum (papal tiara) and he gave for the first time as pope the famous blessing Urbi et Orbi ("to the City [Rome] and to the World"). Another renowned part of the coronation was the lighting of a bundle of flax at the top of a gilded pole, which would flare brightly for a moment and then promptly extinguish, as he said, Sic transit gloria mundi ("Thus passes worldly glory"). A similar warning against papal hubris made on this occasion was the traditional exclamation, "Annos Petri non-videbis", reminding the newly crowned pope that he would not live to see his rule lasting as long as that of St. Peter. According to tradition, he headed the church for 35 years and has thus far been the longest-reigning pope in the history of the Catholic Church.

The Latin term, sede vacante ("while the see is vacant"), refers to a papal interregnum, the period between the death or resignation of a pope and the election of his successor. From this term is derived the term sede vacantism, which designates a category of dissident Catholics who maintain that there is no canonically and legitimately elected pope, and that there is therefore a sede vacante.

For centuries, starting from 1378 onwards, those elected to the papacy were predominantly Italians. Prior to the election of the Polish-born John Paul II in 1978, the last non-Italian was Adrian VI of the Netherlands, elected in 1522. John Paul II was followed by election of the German-born Benedict XVI, who was in turn followed by Argentine-born Francis, the first non-European after 1272 years and the first Latin American (albeit of Italian ancestry).

Death

The current regulations regarding a papal interregnum—that is, a sede vacante ("vacant seat")—were promulgated by Pope John Paul II in his 1996 document Universi Dominici Gregis. During the sede vacante period, the College of Cardinals is collectively responsible for the government of the Church and of the Vatican itself, under the direction of the Camerlengo of the Holy Roman Church. Canon law specifically forbids the cardinals from introducing any innovation in the government of the Church during the vacancy of the Holy See. Any decision that requires the assent of the pope has to wait until the new pope has been elected and accepts office.

In recent centuries, when a pope was judged to have died, it was reportedly traditional for the cardinal camerlengo to confirm the death ceremonially by gently tapping the pope's head thrice with a silver hammer, calling his birth name each time. This was not done on the deaths of popes John Paul I and John Paul II. The cardinal camerlengo retrieves the Ring of the Fisherman and cuts it in two in the presence of the cardinals. The pope's seals are defaced, to keep them from ever being used again, and his personal apartment is sealed. The body lies in state for several days before being interred in the crypt of a leading church or cathedral; all popes who have died in the 20th and 21st centuries have been interred in St. Peter's Basilica. A nine-day period of mourning (novendialis) follows the interment. It is highly unusual for a pope to resign. The 1983 Code of Canon Law states, "If it happens that the Roman Pontiff resigns his office, it is required for validity that the resignation is made freely and properly manifested but not that it is accepted by anyone." Benedict XVI, who vacated the Holy See on 28 February 2013, was the most recent to do so, and the first since Gregory XII's resignation in 1415.

Popes adopt a new name on their accession, known as papal name, in Italian and Latin. Currently, after a new pope is elected and accepts the election, he is asked, "By what name shall you be called?" The new pope chooses the name by which he will be known from that point on. The senior cardinal deacon, or cardinal protodeacon, then appears on the balcony of Saint Peter's to proclaim the new pope by his birth name, and announce his papal name in Latin. It's customary when referring to popes to translate the regnal name into all local languages. For example, the current pope bears the papal name Papa Franciscus in Latin and Papa Francesco in Italian, but Papa Francisco in his native Spanish, Pope Francis in English.

Bishop of Rome, Vicar of Jesus Christ, Successor of the Prince of the Apostles, Supreme Pontiff of the Universal Church, Patriarch of the West, Primate of Italy, Archbishop and Metropolitan of the Roman Province, Sovereign of the Vatican City State, Servant of the servants of God.

The best-known title, that of "pope", does not appear in the official list, but is commonly used in the titles of documents, and appears, in abbreviated form, in their signatures. Thus Paul VI signed as "Paulus PP. VI", the "PP." standing for "papa pontifex" ("pope and pontiff").

The title "pope" was from the early 3rd century an honorific designation used for any bishop in the West. In the East, it was used only for the bishop of Alexandria. Marcellinus (304AD) is the first bishop of Rome shown in sources to have had the title "pope" used of him. From the 6th century, the imperial chancery of Constantinople normally reserved this designation for the bishop of Rome. From the early 6th century, it began to be confined in the West to the bishop of Rome, a practice that was firmly in place by the 11th century.

In Eastern Christianity, where the title "pope" is used also of the bishop of Alexandria, the bishop of Rome is often referred to as the "pope of Rome", regardless of whether the speaker or writer is in communion with Rome or not.

"Vicar of Jesus Christ" (Vicarius Iesu Christi) is one of the official titles of the pope given in the Annuario Pontificio. It is commonly used in the slightly abbreviated form "vicar of Christ" (vicarius Christi).

In the earlier centuries of Christianity, the title "Pope", meaning "father", had been used by all bishops. Some popes used the term and others did not. Eventually, the title became associated especially with the bishop of Rome. In a few cases, the term is used for other Christian clerical authorities. In English, Catholic priests are still addressed as "father", but the term "pope" is reserved for the head of the church hierarchy.

In the Catholic Church

"Black Pope" is a name that was popularly, but unofficially, given to the superior general of the Society of Jesus due to the Jesuits' importance within the Church. This name, based on the black color of his cassock, was used to suggest a parallel between him and the "White Pope" (since the time of Pius V the popes dress in white) and the cardinal prefect of the Congregation for the Evangelization of Peoples (formerly called the Sacred Congregation for the Propagation of the Faith), whose red cardinal's cassock gave him the name of the "Red Pope" in view of the authority over all territories that were not considered in some way Catholic. In the present time this cardinal has power over mission territories for Catholicism, essentially the Churches of Africa and Asia, but in the past his competence extended also to all lands where Protestants or Eastern Christianity was dominant. Some remnants of this situation remain, with the result that, for instance, New Zealand is still in the care of this Congregation.

In the Eastern Churches

Since the papacy of Heraclas in the 3rd century, the bishop of Alexandria in both the Coptic Orthodox Church and the Greek Orthodox Church of Alexandria continues to be called "pope", the former being called "Coptic pope" or, more properly, "Pope and Patriarch of All Africa on the Holy Orthodox and Apostolic Throne of Saint Mark the Evangelist and Holy Apostle" and the latter called "Pope and Patriarch of Alexandria and All Africa".

In the Bulgarian Orthodox Church, Russian Orthodox Church, Serbian Orthodox Church and Macedonian Orthodox Church, it is not unusual for a village priest to be called a "pope" ("поп" pop).

This is different from the words used for the head of the Catholic Church (Bulgarian "папа" papa, Russian "папа римский" papa rimskiy). In new religious movements and other Christian-related new religious movements. Some new religious movements within Christianity, especially those that have disassociated themselves from the Catholic Church yet retain a Catholic hierarchical framework, have used the designation "pope" for a founder or current leader. Examples include the African Legio Maria Church and the European Palmarian Catholic Church in Spain. The Cao Dai, a Vietnamese faith that duplicates the Catholic hierarchy, is similarly headed by a pope. What is the Holy Bible?

It is a REVELATION of God, of the Fall of Man, the Way of Salvation, and of God's "Plan and Purpose in the Ages." (World)

It treats of-
1). Four Persons-God the Father, God the Son, God the Holy Spirit, and Satan. 2).Three Places-Heaven, Earth and Hell. 3).Three Classes of People-The Jew, the Gentile, and the Church of God. The Scriptures were given to us piece-meal, "at sundry times and in divers manners." Holy men of God spoke as they were moved by the Holy Spirit, during a period of 1600 years, extending from B.C. 1492 to A. D. 100. The Bible consists of 66 separate books; 39 in the Old Testament, and 27 in the New Testament. These books were written by about 40 different authors. By kings such as David and Solomon; by statesmen, as Daniel and Nehemiah; by priests, as Ezra; by men learned in the wisdom of Egypt, as Moses; by men learned in Jewish law, as Paul. By a herdsman, Amos; a tax-gatherer, Matthew; fishermen, as Peter, James and John, who were "unlearned and ignorant" men; a physician, Luke; and such mighty "seers" as Isaiah, Ezekiel and Zechariah. It is not an Asiatic book, though it was written in that part of the world. Its pages were penned in the Wilderness of Sinai, the cliffs of Arabia, the hills and towns of Palestine, the courts of the Temple, the schools of the prophets at Bethel and Jericho, in the palace of Shushan in Persia, on the banks of the river Chebar in Babylonia, in the dungeons of Rome, and on the lonely Island of Patmos, in the Aegean Sea. Imagine another book compiled in a similar manner.

Suppose, for illustration, that we take 66 medical books written by 40 different physicians and surgeons during a period of 1600 years, of various schools of medicine, as Allopathy, Homeopathy, Hydropathy, Osteopathy, etc., and bind them all together, and then undertake to doctor a man according to that book, what success would we expect to have, and what accord would there be in such a medical work.

While the Bible has been compiled in the manner described, it is not a "heterogeneous jumble" of ancient history, myths, legends, religious speculations and superstitions. There is a progress of revelation and doctrine in it. The judges knew more than the Patriarchs, the Prophets than the judges, the Apostles than the Prophets. The Old and New Testaments are not separate and distinct books, the New taking the place of the Old they are the two halves of a whole. The New is "enfolded" in the Old, and the Old is "unfolded" in the New.

These books tell us how we can be saved from the evil of this world and gain eternal life that is truly worth living. Although the Holy Bible contains rules of conduct, it is not just a rule book. It reveals God's heart— a Father's heart, full of love and compassion. The Holy Bible tells you what you need to know about the "Spoken Word" first, then believe in what is written about being saved from sin and evil and how to live a life that is truly worth living, no matter what your current circumstances may be. The Holy Bible consists of two main sections: the Old Testament(Spoken Word) (Ancient Of Days) (including Psalms and Proverbs) and the New Testament(the written word) (Matthew through Revelation). The Old Testament records God's spoken word interaction with mankind to know how to redeem us from us, while recording prophesy predicting that coming. The New Testament tells us of God's Son and Anointed One, Jesus Bar Abbas, and the wonderful salvation that He purchased for all mankind. The same Holy Spirit(the Universal female) who inspired the Holy Bible is living among us today, and He is happy to help you understand what He intended as you study His Word. Just ask Him, and He is more than happy to help you apply His message to your life. The Old Testament was spoken in Hebrew language. The New Testament was originally written mostly in the common street Greek (not the formal Greek used for official legal matters). The Holy Bible is being translated into every living language in the World, so that everyone may have an opportunity to know how to live GOD.

WHO WROTE THE BIBLE!!!

The Bible is not a systematic treaty on Theology, or Morals, or History, or Science, or any other topic. It is a REVELATION of GOD, of the Fall of Man, the Way of Salvation, and of GOD's "Plan and Purpose in the Ages." While the Bible has been compiled in the manner described, it is not a "heterogeneous jumble" of ancient history, myths, legends, religious speculations and superstitions. There is a progress of revelation and doctrine in it. The judges knew more than the Patriarchs, the Prophets than the judges and the Apostles than the Prophets. The Old and New Testaments are not separate and distinct books, the New taking the place of the Old they are the two halves of a whole. The New is "enfolded" in the Old, and the Old is "unfolded" in the New. You cannot understand Leviticus of Matthew, Mark, Luke and John. While the Bible is a revelation from God, it is not written in a superhuman or celestial language. If that were it, we could not understand much of it. Its supernatural origin however is seen in the fact that it can be translated into any language and not lose its virility or spiritual life giving power, and when translated into any language it fixes that language in its purest form. The language however of the Bible is of three kinds. A Figurative, Symbolical and Literal, Such expressions as "Harden not your heart," "Let the dead bury their dead," are figurative and their meaning is made clear by context. Symbolic language like the description of Nebuchadnezzar' s "Colossus" Daniel' s "Four Wild Beasts" or Christ in the midst of the "Seven Candlesticks," explained, either in the same chapter, or somewhere else in the Bible. The rest of the language of the Bible is to be interpreted according to the customary rules of grammar and rhetoric. That is, we are to read the Bible as we would read any other book, letting it say what it wants to say, and not allegorical or spiritualize its meaning. It is this false method of interpreting Scripture that has led us to the origin of so many religious sects and denominations. There are three things that we must avoid in the handling of God's Word. 1). The Misinterpretation of Scripture. 2). The Misapplication of Scripture. 3). The Dislocation of Scripture. The basis of men are not willing to allow the Scriptures say what they want to say. This is largely due to their training, environment, prejudice, or desire to make sure the Scriptures teach the proper doctrine.

Then again we must not overlook the "Parabolic Method" of imparting truth. Jesus did not invent it, though He largely used it, it was employed by the Old Testament prophets. In the New Testament it is used as a "Mystery of imparting truth. Matt. 13:10-12. A mystery is not something that cannot be known, but something that for the time being is hidden. I hand you a sealed letter. What it contains is a mystery to you. Break the seal and read the letter and it ceases to be a mystery. But you may not be able to read the letter, because it is written in a language with which you are not familiar. Learn the language and the mystery ceases. But perhaps the letter contains technical terms which you do not understand, learn their meaning and all will be plain. That is the way with the Mysteries of the Scriptures, learn to, read them by the help of their author, the Holy Spirit, and they will no longer be mysteries. This brings us to the great questions-WHO WROTE THE BIBLE? . . . . IS THE BIBLE GOD'S BOOK OR MAN'S BOOK?

That is, did God write it, or is it simply a collection of the writings of men? If it is simply a collection of the writings of men, without any divine guidance, then it is no more reliable than are the writings of men; but if God wrote it, then it must be true, and we can depend upon its statements. It is clear from the character of the Bible that it is not the work of man, for man could not have written it if he would, and would not have written it if he could. The Bible is the no.1 Bestseller in the history of the World since its existence of the 16th century. Being sold at over 6 billion copies and there is only 7 billion people in the World. If Man is so credited for writing the Bible that sold over 6 billion copies, then why can't man write another book to out sell the "The Bible"?

CHAPTER V

Ecclesiastic Law

The Ecclesiastical Law

The one thing the Greeks determine is that information does not transform your life. Why? Because you must first receive it, then accept it, then apply the information before you know it. And at such point it becomes "Law" and that is what transform you, because law commands and demands that you do. Not information. And this is what the written word called bible is powered by the greatest manipulation of law known to mankind on earth called the "Ecclesiastical Law". And so the body of law derived from canon and civil law and administered by the ecclesiastical courts. Ecclesiastical law governs the doctrine of a specific church, usually, Anglican canon law. Ecclesiastical law is also termed as jus ecclesisasticum or law spiritual.

Ecclesiastical courts were established to hear matters concerning the religion. The jurisdiction exercised by ecclesiastical courts played a major role in the development of the English legal system. Their duties and work were not limited to the controlling of clergies and doctrines of the Church. Before the Reformation, the ecclesiastical courts had significant jurisdiction. In matters relating to matrimonial causes and testate and intestate succession, the law remained significant and relevant until the mid of the nineteenth century.

Since ecclesiastical courts were not established in the United States, the code of laws enforced in such courts could not be considered part of the common law that existed in the colonies. It has also been stated that the canon and civil laws administered by the ecclesiastical courts of England should be grouped along with the unwritten laws of England which were adopted and used in certain jurisdiction. Therefore, it is argued that such laws should be employed where the rule of the ecclesiastical courts is deemed to be better law than the rule announced by a common law court.
The canon law of the Catholic Church (from Latin ius canonicum) is "how the Church organizes and governs herself". It is the system of laws and ecclesiastical legal principles made and enforced by the hierarchical authorities of the Catholic Church to regulate its external organization and government and to order and direct the activities of Catholics toward the mission of the Church.

It was the first modern Western legal system and is the oldest continuously functioning legal system in the West, while the unique traditions of Eastern Catholic canon law govern the 23 Eastern Catholic particular churches sui iuris. Positive ecclesiastical laws, based directly or indirectly upon immutable divine law or natural law, derive formal authority in the case of universal laws from promulgation by the supreme legislator—the supreme pontiff, who possesses the totality of legislative, executive, and judicial power in his person, or by the College of Bishops acting in communion with the pope. In contrast, particular laws derive formal authority from promulgation by a legislator inferior to the supreme legislator, whether an ordinary or a delegated legislator. The actual subject material of the canons is not just doctrinal or moral in nature, but all-encompassing of the human condition.

The canon law of the Catholic Church has all the ordinary elements of a mature legal system: laws, courts, lawyers, judges. The canon law of the Catholic Church is articulated in the legal code for the Latin Church[9] as well as a code for the Eastern Catholic Churches. This canon law has principles of legal interpretation, and coercive penalties. It lacks civilly-binding force in most secular jurisdictions. Those who are versed and skilled in canon law, and professors of canon law, are called canonists (or colloquially, canon lawyers). Canon law as a sacred science is called canonistics.

The jurisprudence of canon law is the complex of legal principles and traditions within which canon law operates, while the philosophy, theology, and fundamental theory of Catholic canon law are the areas of philosophical, theological, and legal scholarship dedicated to providing a theoretical basis for canon law as a legal system and as true law.

The term "canon law" (ius canonicum) was only regularly used from the twelfth century onwards. The term ius ecclesiasticum, by contrast, referred to the secular law, whether imperial, royal, or feudal, that dealt with relations between the state and the Catholic Church. The term corpus iuris canonici was used to denote canon law as legal system beginning in the thirteenth century.

Other terms sometimes used synonymously with ius canonicum include ius sacrum, ius ecclesiasticum, ius divinum, and ius pontificium, as well as sacri canones (sacred canons).

Ecclesiastical positive law is the positive law that emanates from the legislative power of the Catholic Church in its effort to govern its members in accordance with the Gospel of Jesus Christ. Fernando della Rocca used the term "ecclesiastical-positive law" in contradistinction to civil-positive law, in order to differentiate between the human legislators of church and state, all of which issue "positive law" in the normal sense.

The word "canon" comes from the Greek kanon, which in its original usage denoted a straight rod, was later used for a measuring stick, and eventually came to mean a rule or norm. In 325AD, when the first ecumenical council, Nicaea I, was held, kanon started to obtain the restricted juridical denotation of a law promulgated by a synod or ecumenical council, as well as that of an individual bishop.

The term source or fountain of canon law (fons iuris canonici) may be taken in a twofold sense: a) as the formal cause of the existence of a law, and in this sense of the fontes essendi (Latin: "sources of being") of canon law or lawgivers; b) as the material channel through which laws are handed down and made known, and in this sense the sources are styled fontes cognoscendi (Latin: "sources of knowing"), or depositaries, like sources of history.

The Catholic Church has the oldest continuously functioning legal system in the West, much later than Roman law but predating the evolution of modern European civil law traditions. What began with rules ("canons") said to have been adopted by the Apostles at the Council of Jerusalem in the first century has developed into a highly complex legal system encapsulating not just norms of the New Testament, but some elements of the Hebrew (Old Testament), Roman, Visigothic, Saxon, and Celtic legal traditions. As many as 36 collections of canon law are known to have been brought into existence before 1150AD. The history of Latin canon law can be divided into four periods: the ius antiquum, the ius novum, the ius novissimum and the Codex Iuris Canonici.

In relation to the Code, history can be divided into the ius vetus (all law before the 1917 Code) and the ius novum (the law of the code, or ius codicis).

The Eastern Catholic canon law of the Eastern Catholic Churches, which had developed some different disciplines and practices, underwent its own process of codification, resulting in the Code of Canons of the Eastern Churches promulgated in 1990 by Pope John Paul II.

St. Raymond of Penyafort (1175–1275), a Spanish Dominican priest, is the patron saint of canonists, due to his important contributions to canon law in codifying the Decretales Gregorii IX. Other saintly patrons include St. Ivo of Chartres and the Jesuit St. Robert Bellarmine.

In the Early Church, the first canons were decreed by bishops united in "Ecumenical" councils (the Emperor summoning all of the known world's bishops to attend with at least the acknowledgement of the Bishop of Rome) or "local" councils (bishops of a region or territory). Over time, these canons were supplemented with decretals of the Bishops of Rome, which were responses to doubts or problems according to the maxim, "Roma locuta est, causa finita est" ("Rome has spoken, the case is closed"). A common misconception, the Catholic Encyclopedia links this saying to St Augustine who actually said something quite different: "jam enim de hac causa duo concilia missa sunt ad sedem apostolicam; inde etiam rescripta venerunt; causa finita est" (which roughly translate to: "there are two councils, for now, this matter as brought to the Apostolic See, whence also letters are come to pass, the case was finished") in response to the heretical Pelagianism of the time.

In the first millennium of the Latin Church, the canons of various ecumenical and local councils were supplemented with decretals of the popes; these were gathered together into collections. The period of canonical history known as the Ius novum ("new law") or middle period covers the time from Gratian to the Council of Trent (mid-12th century– 16th century).

The spurious conciliar canons and papal decrees were gathered together into collections, both unofficial and official. In the year 1000, there was no book that had attempted to summarize the whole body of canon law, to systematize it in whole or in part. The first truly systematic collection was assembled by the Camaldolese monk Gratian in the 11th century, commonly known as the Decretum Gratiani ("Gratian's Decree") but originally called The Concordance of Discordant Canons (Concordantia Discordantium Canonum). Before Gratian there was no "jurisprudence of canon law" (system of legal interpretation and principles). Gratian is the founder of canonical jurisprudence, which merits him the title "Father of Canon Law". Gratian also had an enormous influence on the history of natural law in his transmission of the ancient doctrines of natural law to Scholasticism.

Canon law greatly increased from 1140AD to 1234AD. After that, it slowed down, except for the laws of local councils (an area of canon law in need of scholarship), and secular laws supplemented. In 1234AD Pope Gregory IX promulgated the first official collection of canons, called the Decretalia Gregorii Noni or Liber Extra. This was followed by the Liber Sextus (1298AD) of Boniface VIII, the Clementines (1317AD) of Clement V, the Extravagantes Joannis XXII and the Extravagantes Communes, all of which followed the same structure as the Liber Extra. All these collections, with the Decretum Gratiani, are together referred to as the Corpus Iuris Canonici. After the completion of the Corpus Iuris Canonici, subsequent papal legislation was published in periodic volumes called Bullaria.

In the thirteenth century, the Roman Church began to collect and organize its canon law, which after a millennium of development had become a complex and difficult system of interpretation and cross-referencing. The official collections were the Liber Extra (1234AD) of Pope Gregory IX, the Liber Sextus (1298AD) of Boniface VIII and the Clementines (1317AD), prepared for Clement V but published by John XXII. These were addressed to the universities by papal letters at the beginning of each collection, and these texts became textbooks for aspiring canon lawyers. In 1582AD a compilation was made of the Decretum, Extra, the Sext, the Clementines, and the Extravagantes (that is, the decretals of the popes from Pope John XXII to Pope Sixtus IV).

From the days of Ethelbert onwards [say, from the year 600], English law was under the influence of so much of Roman law as had worked itself into the traditions of the Catholic Church. Much of the legislative style was adapted from that of Roman Law especially the Justinianic Corpus Iuris Civilis. After the 'fall' of the Roman Empire and up until the revival of Roman Law in the 11th century canon law served as the most important unifying force among the local systems in the Civil Law tradition. The Catholic Church developed the inquisitorial system in the Middle Ages. The canonists introduced into post-Roman Europe the concept of a higher law of ultimate justice, over and above the momentary law of the state.

In one of his elaborate orations in the United States Senate Mr. Charles Sumner spoke of "the generous presumption of the common law in favor of the innocence of an accused person" yet it must be admitted that such a presumption cannot be found in Anglo-Saxon law, where sometimes the presumption seems to have been the other way. And in a very recent case in the Supreme Court of the United States, the case of Coffin, 156 U. S. 432, it is pointed out that this presumption was fully established in the Roman law, and was preserved in the canon law.

The primary canonical sources of law are the 1983 Code of Canon Law, the Code of Canons of the Eastern Churches and Pastor Bonus. Other sources include apostolic constitutions, motibus propriis, particular law, and—with the approbation of the competent legislator—custom. A law must be promulgated for it to have legal effect. A later and contrary law obrogates an earlier law. Canonists have formulated interpretive rules of law for the magisterial (non-legislatorial) interpretation of canon laws. An authentic interpretation is an official interpretation of a law issued by the law's legislator, and has the force of law.

CHAPTER VI

The Image of Cesare Borgia

Cesare Borgia His Life and Times

Between 1502 and 1503, he employed Leonardo da Vinci as a military architect and engineer in which him and Leonardo da Vinci became intimate instantaneously, they were lovers. To express his love towards Cesare, Leonardo painted many pictures of him. Cesare's Father Rodrigo Borgia, who later became Pope Alexander VI, under the authority of the Catholic Church Elite, had his son picture put up as Jesus Christ in the Western World. Cesare had sex with his own sister Lucrezia, and he killed his brother Giovanni in 1497, and this is the man whom the Catholic Church gave their consent to allowing his picture to be put up and portrayed as Jesus Christ to deceive the whole world to think Christ was European. See what most people don't know is, there was a competition during the time called the Renaissance period, between Leonardo da Vinci and the well known Michelangelo. The competition was to see who could impress the king by a making a new image of the King's son that would deceive the world, in which Leonardo da Vinci won the competition. The original King James Bible of 1611 had the Apocrypha in it, but in 1928 under the Vatican, they made an agreement to take 14 books out of the King James holy bible. Why you might ask, well because thousands of years before they put this image up to be Christ, they found out that it was written off in the Wisdom of Solomon located in the Apocrypha, that they would do this and the reason for it. So knowing this was written off in the Wisdom of Solomon, the Roman Catholic Church took it out of the bible so the people wouldn't figure out their deception. It is a noted fact that when they did this, they knew exactly what Christ people really looked like, they knew Christ and his people were not Europeans, but instead were actually Hebrews, who were dark brown people. So let's find out in the bible first what Satan was going to do, and then will find out what exactly was written in the Wisdom of Solomon that the Apocrypha had to be taken out and credited as unscriptural and not divinely inspired, by the Catholic Church. So what is written off in the bible that Satan would do? Revelation 12:9; And the great dragon was cast out, that old serpent, called the Devil, and Satan, which deceived the whole world: he was cast out into the earth, and his angels were cast out with him.

So it is written that Satan would deceive the whole world, in which he is doing this through the Catholic Church and through the so called children of God called the Jews, who are really the children of Satan according to Revelation 2:9 and 3:9. So now we know Satan plan is to deceive the whole world and we know that through the Catholic Church and the so called Jews are whom he is using to execute his plan. So now let's examine what was written in the Apocrypha that was so critical to our knowledge, that it had to be taken out and defamed as being unbiblical and not divinely inspired. This image that we see is said to be Christ and is portrayed all over the world as Christ, but says the word of God about it? Wisdom of Solomon 14:8; But that which is made with hands is cursed, as well it, as he that made it: he, because he made it; and it, because, being corruptible, it was called god. Scripture says that which is made with hands is cursed, but why would it be so? Isaiah 2:8 - Their land also is full of idols; they worship the work of their own hands, that which their own fingers have made: Because the image that they put up, they called it Christ, which therefore it not being Christ made it a curse and a sin unto them because they themselves made it with their own hands and fingers. So therefore by calling it Christ, they give glory unto another and not the true and living God, therefore they worship it and give honor to it as being God which makes it idolatry. So being corruptible, this image was called God, so when the true people would begin to desire to learn about Christ, they would be told they worship this guy, then they would ask who is he, and they would be told he's Christ. What else is written?

Wisdom of Solomon 14:9; For the ungodly and his ungodliness are both alike hateful unto God. Wisdom of Solomon 14:10 - For that which is made shall be punished together with him that made it. So the image that the Catholic Church allowed to be put up as Christ will be destroyed, and also them and everyone who had a hand in pushing this deception unto the people, so there is a judgment awaiting them. They didn't do this to be nice, they had a motive behind pushing this deception which was mentally driving them to push a belief into the mindset of the people, in which they were pushing this during the Renaissance period. So now knowing that this image is idolatry and an idol of the heathens, what else is written about this? Wisdom of Solomon 14:11; Therefore even upon the idols of the Gentiles shall there be a visitation: because in the creature of God they are become an abomination, and stumbling blocks to the souls of men, and a snare to the feet of the unwise.

So by them doing this, they are an abomination unto God because in doing so, this image would become a stumbling block to the souls of men, and a snare to the feet of the unwise, how so? Because they knew Christ and his people wasn't European, so they knew that if they put up images of European people, then the true people would think the images are actually the people they are reading of in the bible. They knew they would open their bibles and see all these images of people who didn't resemble their skin color, but yet would see their family following this man who is suppose to be Christ, and see them believing that the people in these images were actually the people of Christ, and would feel excluded from the bible. So then they knew the true people would vary away from the bible and lose interest in it because they would consider it to be the white's man book, which this was part of their plan it's psychology at its best form. Because without a race having any biblical connection to coincide with their spirituality, they therefore will have no identity which would reverse their perception of self into a form of hatred towards others of their skin tone.

Which is why black on black crime is high, because they can't look at each other and see they are one, which is also why our people learn to hate themselves and fight each other, but love all those who hate them, thus creating a stumbling block to the souls of men. So in the creation of this image and other images portraying Christ and his people as European, what came from this? Wisdom of Solomon 14:12; For the devising of idols was the beginning of spiritual fornication, and the invention of them the corruption of life. Wisdom of Solomon 14:13; For neither were they from the beginning, neither shall they be forever. So in creating the false images of Christ and his people as Europeans, and worshipping them as Christ and his people doing so was the beginning of spiritual fornication. Why, because now when the people are not yet of Christ but learning of him, they are actually loving other gods whom the people aren't espoused to, so therefore they cheating on the true Christ with other gods spiritually, because they giving them time and love and affection and praise and worship as if they are the true Christ. But these images weren't here in the beginning, and neither shall they remain upon the earth forever. So how did these false images get here?

The Apocrypha Book Wisdom of Solomon
Wisdom of Solomon 14:14 - For by the vain glory of men they entered into the world, and therefore shall they come shortly to an end. Scripture says by the vain glory of men these images entered into the world, and surely they shall soon come to amend in this world. So where does Cesare Borgia and his father Rodrigo Borgia come in the picture? Wisdom of Solomon 14:15 - For a father afflicted with untimely mourning, when he hath made an image of his child soon taken away, now honored him as a god, which was then a dead man, and delivered to those that were under him ceremonies and sacrifices. Reference to his son Cesare, image put up to be Christ, which is how they honored him as a God though he was unknown at the time in Rome, thus making him dead.

They used this false image of Cesare as Christ, and they brought forth a false teaching and ceremonies and sacrifices and holidays all along with this image, to deceive the people to believe these things were of this guy whom they were portraying as Christ. So what else came along with this the false Christ? Wisdom of Solomon 14:16; Thus in process of time an ungodly custom grown strong was kept as a law, and graven images were worshipped by the commandments of kings. From this false image, an ungodly custom grown strong was kept as a law, and that custom was Christmas, in which they told you it was the birthday of Christ. And they made Jesus pictures and Mary pictures and crosses and all forms of idolatry to resemble biblical things to appear European to support their demonic intentions. What else is written?

Wisdom of Solomon 14:17; Whom men could not honor in presence, because they dwelt far off, they took the counterfeit of his visage from far, and made an express image of a king whom they honored, to the end that by this their forwardness they might flatter him that was absent, as if he were present. Not everybody could honor this guy in the image as Christ in person, because some of the people lived far away. So they took this false image of Christ back to their native lands with them, and they made unto themselves images of other gods whom they could honor closely, so that they may worship their respective god in the images as if they were present. What did the people do? 2 Kings 17:29; Howbeit every nation made gods of their own, and put them in the houses of the high places which the Samaritans had made, every nation in their cities wherein they dwelt. Proved that!

Question: What else is written? Wisdom of Solomon 14:18; Also the singular diligence of the artificer did help to set forward the ignorant to more superstition. Wisdom of Solomon 14:19; For he, peradventure willing to please one in authority, forced all his skill to make the resemblance of the best fashion. Now remember the competition during the time called the Renaissance period, between Leonardo da Vinci and the well known Michelangelo, was to see who could impress the king by a making a new image of the King's son that would deceive the world, in which Leonardo da Vinci won. So by him winning and creating with his hands this false image of Christ, he set forward those who had no knowledge of this, meaning he caused them to have an irrational belief arising from ignorance of not knowing who this guy is that they are really worshipping. So Leonardo being willing to please Rodrigo Borgia, the Pope in authority at the time also the father of Cesare Borgia, he compelled all this talent to make the image resemble his son Cesare Borgia in the best way possible. What else is written?

Wisdom of Solomon 14:20; And so the multitude, allured by the grace of the work, took him now for a god, which a little before was but honored. Wisdom of Solomon 14:21; And this was an occasion to deceive the world: for men, serving either calamity or tyranny, did ascribe unto stones and stocks the incommunicable name. So after impressing him, the multitude of people were drawn by the elegance and beauty of this image, and accepted it and took it to be their God, which beforehand wasn't revered by all as a God. And the reason they did this, was to deceive the world, and men begin to attribute this image and give credit to it, by not revealing to others who this guy is that's suppose to be God, thus fulfilling Revelation 12:9; And the great dragon was cast out, that old serpent, called the Devil, and Satan, which deceives the whole world: he was cast out into the earth, and his angels were cast out with him.

So Satan with the help of the Catholic Church has deceived the whole world into thinking this image is Christ, when it's really Cesare Borgia. What did Satan say? Isaiah 14:14; I will ascend above the heights of the clouds; I will be like the most High. So through this false image of Christ, Satan gets the glory as if he was God, like he said. So now you see why the Catholic Church took the Apocrypha out of the holy bible, they didn't want to get exposed, but little did they know I would come along one day.

1. The whole world is deceived, they got this image on movies, cds and dvds, t shirts, keychains, necklaces, bracelets, ornaments, stockings, pictures, coffee mugs, pens, air fresheners, wrist bands, watches, rugs, bill boards, windows, and even tattooed on their body, thinking it's Christ when really it's Cesare Borgia. So what should the people know and do? Deuteronomy 4:15; Take therefore good heed to yourselves; for you saw no manner of similitude on the day that the LORD spoke to you in Horeb out of the midst of the fire: Ask yourself, if the people didn't see no image of Christ, but only heard the voice of the words, then how did they know what he looked like? Yet, the images that were given by the Catholic Church are supposed to be Christ, but yet they don't look as how the bible says Christ looked. Why should they take good heed, what if they make them a similitude and say it's Christ? Deuteronomy 4:16; Less you corrupt yourselves, and make you a graven image, the similitude of any figure, the likeness of male or female, Deuteronomy 4:15 warned us to take heed because we never saw what Christ looked like, and Deuteronomy 4:16 tells us why, because if we make ourselves a graven image, the similitude of any figure, the likeness of male or female, we are corrupted. What is a graven image? Graven Image a material effigy that is worshipped as a god. So those who have the blonde hair blue eyed picture who is suppose to be Christ, and those who have the black face dredlock hair picture who is suppose to be Christ, and those who have any picture that is supposed to be Christ, you are corrupted and an idolatry worshipper.

Bible describes Christ and his people as people of color, but that doesn't give no one the right to make an image of what the bible says they look like. What else does the scripture say? 1 John 4:12; No man has seen God at any time. If we love one another, God dwelled in us, and his love is perfected in us. No man have seen God at anytime, so how is it that the world has pictures who they say is God, and believes they are God, despite the scripture saying no man hath seen God at anytime? Revelation 12:9; And the great dragon was cast out, that old serpent, called the Devil, and Satan, which deceives the whole world: he was cast out into the earth, and his angels were cast out with him. Because the devil has deceived the whole world! Any pastor who has a picture that is supposed to be Christ in the church, or home in society as being Christ, he is wrong, simple.

2 Corinthians 4:13; It is written: "I believed; therefore I have spoken." Since we have that same spirit of faith, we also believe and therefore speak, we believe, therefore we speak what's written, so if it's not written that Christ was white with blonde hair and blue eyes, then how do you have faith if what you believe is not written? You not even saved!

Humus Soil

So how did God create man and what did he look like? Genesis 2: 6; But there went up a mist from the earth, and watered the whole face of the ground. When water gets on the ground, it makes the soil fertile in which when something is fertile, it is able to produce an offspring because it's capable of reproducing. For example, a woman can't just have a baby she has to be fertile first and she becomes fertile by first, ovulating which then she ripens and releases an egg or eggs from the ovary for possible fertilization. So God ripen and released water onto the ground to make it fertile to produce an offspring. So now that the ground, which is soil, is able to reproduce or give life, what did God do next?

Genesis 2:7; And the LORD God formed man of the dust of the ground, and breathed into his nostrils the breath of life; and man became a living soul. So from the soil of the ground, God formed man and breathed into his nostrils the breath of life, and man became a living soul. The garden of Egypt is located in Northern East Africa in which today its existence and location is known as the Fertile Crescent, because of its nutrients in the soil that makes it so fertile to give life to plants and other things. Humus is an organic component of soil which is mostly found in Northern East Africa. It is a dark brown organic component of soil that improves the water-retaining properties of soil, making it more fertile and workable. If color didn't matter, then it wouldn't have been described in the bible, and when John turned, he would have said I didn't see any color, I just see Christ, as to what should be said today's society. But the color of his skin is not what's going to save us Hebrews or the gentiles; it is by way of the Holy Spirit of God in receiving the gift of Salvation that is what saves us.

The Hebraic Image

The name Jesus is precious to hundreds of millions of Christians worldwide.

Through a series of circumstances, events and mistakes, the name of the Messiah of Holy Scriptures has been passed down to us as Jesus. Sincere Christians worship the Savior by using that name, sing praises to that name and call upon that name Jesus for salvation and deliverance. The common rendering of Philippians 2:10, 11 underscores the reason for this love of the name Jesus: that at the name of Jesus every knee should bow, of those in heaven, those on earth, and those under the earth, and that every tongue should confess that Jesus Christ is Lord, to the glory of God the Father (TKESB). It is right that sincere worshippers of the Messiah and our Savior should desire to call upon his name and praise his name and sing to his name. But, in the words of the prophet Jeremiah, "surely our fathers have inherited lies" (16:19). The true name of the Messiah has not been faithfully delivered to this generation of believers. In fact, for many centuries, the name of the Messiah of Scripture has been mistakenly rendered Jesus and many have been deceived as to the real name of the One whom we all want to adore and worship. What is the name of the Messiah? Although the popular English rendering is Jesus, we know that cannot actually be his name. Other cultures pronounce his name in a way that is congruous with their own languages. What's in a name? Does it matter that the Messiah is called by so many different names? You decide after you consider the following information....Why is the Messiah's Name Rendered Jesus In Our Bibles? The faith as put forth in the New Testament Christian Scriptures is centered upon one individual. This man is presented as the Messiah, who was the promised One of the Hebrew Scriptures, who was to come and bring salvation to the world and fulfill all the promises made to the patriarchs. Most English Bibles use the name Jesus when translating the Greek name used in the New Testament Scriptures for the Messiah. But there is a considerable problem with using this name to call upon and refer to the Messiah of the Bible. At the heart of the problem with using the name Jesus as a reference to the Messiah is that the name Jesus wasn't and isn't his real name. The historical Nazarene was a Hebrew. He was Jewish, born of Jewish parents. He and his parents and all Israel during those times spoke Hebrew as their primary language. Therefore, he was given a Hebrew name. But the name Jesus is not a Hebrew name. There is no name even close to sounding like Jesus in Hebrew. Therefore, it is easy to see that the name Jesus is not derived from the Hebrew language. In fact, it is a name derived from the Greek language.

It is a common practice for foreigners coming over to the United States to substitute their own given name for a similar sounding English name. This practice is most notable with Indians coming over to work in the U.S. The Indians typically have very long names which English speaking people have great difficulty pronouncing. So the Indians accommodate us by taking on a much shorter and more common English name in order to fit in more easily. This is also true of people of many other nationalities. It's much easier for everyone to be able to associate a common name with a person. The name Jesus has come to us in this manner.The Hebrew name given at birth to the Messiah was [vwhy(transliterated YHUShA). The reason we know this is that the Messiah's name as given in the Greek New. Testament is the same name as Joshua son of Nun, as indicated by the usage of this same Greek name in Hebrews 4:8. The name for Joshua, when rendered into the Septuagint Greek text is VIhsou, the same name in the Greek New Testament which is rendered Jesus by our English Bibles. So what happened was this: YHUShA, the given Hebrew name of Joshua and of the Messiah was rendered VIhsou/j (I-ay-sous) in the Greek text, because the closest Greek name to the Hebrew YHUShA was I-ay-sous. From the Greek VIhsou/j the English Bible translators took the first Greek letter "I" and rendered it "J" (which was actually a normal thing to do in that day). The "ay" sound got shortened to an "e" sound. And the "sous" ending was shortened to "sus". Putting it together, the Hebrew "Yahusha" became in Greek "I-ay-sous" and then into English as "Jesus".

Why is Jesus as the Name for the Messiah a Problem?

The name Jesus came innocently enough. But there is a huge problem with this name. The root, derivation and meaning of the name Jesus should be startling, even distressing to those who profess a genuine and sincere faith in the Master. The angel told his mother Miriam that the name given to the baby was to be because he would "save his people from their sins" (Matthew 1:21). This is what the Hebrew name [vwhy means - "Yahu saves." But the name Jesus certainly does not have this same meaning. To ascertain the origin and meaning of the name Jesus, we need first to take a glance at the form of the name. There are several other names which share a resemblance to the form (spelling) of this name. Dionysus and Bacchus are well known pagan Greek deities which share the ending of the name Jesus.

This is our first clue. Secondly, the Greek name used in the New Testament manuscripts is transliterated "I-ay-sous" or "yah-sous." This "sous" ending on the Greek name attributed to the Messiah is identical in sound to Dionysous, who is also known in ancient literature as the "sin-bearing son of Zeus." The name Dionysous is fashioned after his father's name Zeus, the Greek super god and father of the pantheon. For this reason, many language experts believe that the name Jesus actually originated from a form of the name of the pagan Greek god Zeus, and not from the Hebrew name referred to in Scripture. The "Iay" which forms the first part of the Greek Iaysous is possibly a reference to another Greek deity Iay, the goddess of healing. The Greek name Iaysous, then, is probably a combination of the names of these two Greek gods, Iay and Zeus. This could roughly be translated as "Zeus is healer." (Others suggest a different source word for "Iay" which would render the meaning of this name as "hail, Zeus" or "praise Zeus.") It was uncovered that the Satanic counterfeiting of Dionysus, son of Zeus for the true son of Elohim, who takes away the sin of the world:

Now, this Babylonian god, known in Greece as "the sin-bearer," and in India as the "Victim-Man," among the Buddhists of the East, the original elements of system are clearly Babylonian, was commonly addressed as the "Savior of the world." It has been all along well enough known that the Greeks occasionally worshiped the supreme god under the title of "Zeus the Savior." When it is known that "Zeus the Savior" was only a title of Dionysus, the "sin bearing Bacchus," his character, as "The Savior," appears in quite a different light.The link uncovered between the pagan savior and sin-bearer with the name attributed to the biblical Savior and sin-bearer, in light of the similarity in the names of each, suggests that the Greek name Iaysous and its corresponding English transliteration, Jesus, are directly related to and derived from the Greek god Zeus and his son Dionysous, vwhy (Yahusha) is the Messiah's Hebrew language name - the name that was given him at birth by his Hebrew speaking parents - the name that was given for him to his mother by the angel. The name Yahusha is the Hebrew name of the Old Testament man known as "Joshua." This name means, "Yahu saves" or "Yahu helps." It should not minimize the effect that the Greek language and culture, which was the mainstream language and culture of that day, had on the propagation of the message Messiah brought to his disciples.

As the faith in Messiah's atoning sacrifice was proclaimed and receiving in the pagan Greek world, it was natural that the Greek mind-set and culture would influence the way those converts expressed their faith. In places where there wasn't a strong history and foundation of Torah study and understanding, the Greek mindset and culture would make inroads into the way converts would live their lives. So, the Greek "equivalent" name Iaysous, because he (Dionysus) was also a "sin-bearing Son of God", would have been thought to be an acceptable and more palatable alternative to the Hebrew name Yahusha for the believing Greek community. In fact, what has really happened is as follows: The early community of believers was influenced by a number of factors as outlined in books like, From Sabbath To Sunday, to change their form of worship from a strictly scriptural model based upon the teaching of Yahusha and the Torah, to a radically different form of worship modeled after the pagan sun-god worship of Mithraism.

Just as Constantine changed the scriptural seventh-day Sabbath to first-day Sun worship, the scriptural holy days into the pagan holidays of Christmas and Easter, and the Torah based walk of faith into a de-Judaized anti-Torah lifestyle, even the very name of the Messiah was stripped of its Hebraic roots and source (Yahusha) and was paganized and Hellenized into the form which is fashioned after the name of their supreme deity Zeus (Sous) and his son, Dionyzeus (Dionysous). And in its final form it became Iayzeus (Iaysous). Then, unwitting English Bible translators transliterated the Greek Iayzeus (Iaysous) into Jesus.

I, for one, do not want to be addressing the set-apart Savior by the name which honors the pagan Greek god Zeus or anything similar to it. I believe that no one else who shares this precious faith in the Creator would want to call Elohim by the name of any pagan god, either. It is time for all true and genuine believers in the Hebrew and Christian Scriptures and in the Messiah to cast behind them the lies that our fathers have inherited and passed on down to us. It's time to repent of these wrong ways of worshipping our Creator and to return to the true understanding of our biblical fathers, Avraham, Yitzchak and Ya'acov. Let's start calling upon the Savior of the world by his real name. Let's address him by his true name - the name Yahusha.

Messiah's Hebrew Birth Name - [vwhy]

To their credit, congregations of the Sacred Name Movement have desired to call upon the Messiah by his given Hebrew name. They understand, correctly, that He was not given a Greek name ("Iaysous" or Jesus) at birth. But, that in fact, he was given a Hebrew name which was well known and was in common usage at that time. The birth account in the book of Mattityahu (Matthew) tells us that "he shall be called VIhsou/j for he shall save his people from their sins" (1:21).

The Greek manuscripts have the name VIhsou/j which is rendered Jesus in most English language Bible translations. But we know that his true name was not the Greek name VIhsou/j because he was a Hebrew Jew. What then is his Hebrew name? How can we be sure? A little bit of analysis of the available data and a little bit of reason will lead us to the correct answer. First of all, whatever his true Hebrew name is, it must have the meaning of the explanation given by the angel to his mother Miriam (Mary). She was told, "for he shall save his people from their sins." In the Hebrew language and culture, particularly in ancient times, names were given to children which related to the circumstances of their birth, or after a relative, or a name with some prophetic significance. Thus, the meaning of the child's name has something to do with "saving his people from their sins." Secondly, let it be noted that the Greek name VIhsou/j is used some 916 times in reference to the Messiah, is also used in the New Testament as a reference to the one we know as Joshua son of Nun. In Hebrews 4:8 we are told that "if VIhsou/j had given them rest, He would not have spoken of another day after those things." The context indicates that he is referring to Joshua son of Nun. Of significance is that the name VIhsou/j was used here to render into Greek the Hebrew name for Joshua. In fact, in the Septuagint, which is the Greek translation of the Hebrew Tanach, the name VIhsou/j is always used to translate Joshua's Hebrew name (a few of those times, there is a slight difference in the spelling of the name). The Hebrew name of Joshua non of Nun is (pronounced Yehoshua) in the Masoretic rabbinic Hebrew text. By unanimous consent, it is agreed that this name has the meaning of "Yahu saves" or "Yahu helps." Thus, we have agreement in the evidence of the usage of VIhsou/j to translate the name of Joshua, and the meaning of the name of Joshua.

This evidence points to the irrefutable conclusion that the Hebrew name of the Messiah is the same as the Hebrew name of the man we call Joshua. When the Messianic Movement began to attract Jews to the Messiah, the name "Yeshua" was adopted as the acceptable Hebrew name for the Messiah, rather than the offensive, Hellenistically derived Jesus. (It is offensive to refer to the true Messiah using the name of a pagan deity.) The word "Yeshua," in the Hebrew tongue, is the generic term usually translated "salvation." Unfortunately, this is not the name given to the babe who was born in the succah in Bethlehem and placed in the animals' feeding trough (manger). Sacred Name groups which sprang up out of the Messianic Movement, who were not concerned with the rabbinic traditions and restrictions which still handcuff the Messianic Jews, were more interested in ascertaining the actual name of the Messiah. His name came to be rendered Yahshua, Yahushua, YaOwHuSHuA, YWHWSHUA, and by others. Each of these representations by Sacred Name groups has been honest and reverent attempts to accurately pronounce Messiah's given human name. We have no criticism for anyone who uses these renderings and pronunciations. However none of those renderings accurately vocalize the Hebrew name [vwhy]. Hebrew is helpful to understand Jesus and His ministry. The people that Jesus ministered to and worked with were mostly Hebrew. Although Jesus would have known several languages, his primary language was Hebrew. Jesus used common rabbinical teaching methods in His teachings, such as the frequent use of the hyperbole like the illustration of having plank of wood or a "SPECK OF SAWDUST" in an eye Mt 7:3-5 (NI) or the suggestion of a camel going through the "EYE OF A NEEDLE" Mt 19:24 (TKESB). Jesus says, "THIS CUP IS THE NEW COVENANT IN MY BLOOD; DO THIS, WHENEVER YOU DRINK IT, IN REMEMBRANCE OF ME" 1 Co 11:25 (NI). These words made sense to some of the Jewish people Jesus was speaking to, if not at the time, and then later after His blood was shed at His crucifixion. Some understood that blood was important in a covenant between God and man. Some understood that a blood sacrifice offering of a lamb was normal in Abraham's day (Ge 22:7-8) and at the time of the Passover (Ex 12:3-21) and in Temple worship (Lev 9:3). Some connected these facts when John the baptizer saw Jesus and referred to Him as, "the Lamb of God, who takes away the sin of the world" (Jn 1:29 NI).

Unfortunately, many Jewish people did not understand as God complained about people who hear but do not "UNDERSTAND"(Is 6:9), including some Jewish followers of Jesus who subsequently stopped following Him after His comments about blood (Jn 6:53-66).

Understanding Jesus' words

Most of Jesus words are easy to translate and understand. A few words may be confusing and difficult to understand and comparing different translations may help, if they are available. Some languages may have more accurate translations than those available in English. For accurate translations, intellectually ability and education and a good communication relationship with God and with His Son Jesus are all important, as both God and Jesus are still alive. The best way to understand what is in the bible is to use the bible to understand what is recorded in the bible. When Jesus words spoken in Hebrew were translated and recorded in Greek the only dictionary available was the Greek translation of the Hebrew bible, the Septuagint, which frequently used a single Greek word for several different Hebrew words. When Jesus says "FOR MANY ARE CALLED, BUT FEW ARE CHOSEN" (Mt 22:14 (TKESB), the word chosen may lead to confusion. The Greek word eklektos, which is, translated "chosen", when we check it in the Septuagint and refer to the original Hebrew word for better understanding; we find eklektos is the Greek translation for over 20 different Hebrew words. For example, in Genesis 41:2 the Hebrew word bari, translated eklektos, refers to the "choice" cows; in Judges 20:16 the Hebrew word bachuwr, also translated eklektos, refers to "select" men or soldiers; in Isaiah 22:7 the Hebrew word mibchar, also translated eklektos, refers to the "most beautiful" or "nicest" valleys; in Isaiah 43:20 the Hebrew word bachiyr, also translated eklektos, refers to God's "chosen" people. Jesus was saying many are "called" but few are "choice, special, extra nice" or "chosen". Many people "ARE CALLED, BUT FEW ARE SPECIAL"(Mt 22:14 (ET). Another example is when Jesus said, "HE WHO BELIEVES IN ME WILL DO THE SAME THINGS THAT I DO. HE WILL DO EVEN GREATER THINGS THAN THESE BECAUSE I AM GOING TO THE FATHER" Jn 14:12 (IC). The word "GREATER" is confusing because what could be greater than all the miracles or works Jesus did?

What can be greater than raising a person for the dead or walking on water or healing people of conditions from birth or being totally guided by God, etc. The Greek word, meizon, translated "greater" in English is used for over 24 Hebrew words in the Septuagint. One of the Hebrew words, gadol, that is translated as meizon in Greek and translated "greater" in English many times but just like in English we have words with more than one meaning, it is also is translated as "more than I can bear" in Ge 4:13 (NI) and as "became more and more powerful" in Est 9:4 (NI). Doing "MORE" than Jesus did in His three years of ministry may be more accurate and more understandable than greater. Another example of a confusing translation is when Jesus after describing the details or events of His second "COMING" states "THIS GENERATION WILL BY NO MEANS PASS AWAY TILL ALL THESE THINGS TAKE PLACE" in Mk 13:30 (NKJ). Obviously the Jewish generation of people Jesus was talking to almost two thousand years ago has passed away. The Greek word for generation, "genea", is correctly translated from the Greek but it was used for ten Hebrew words when the Hebrew. Was translated to the Greek in the Septuagint. "Moledeth" is a Hebrew word found in Genesis 31:3 and 43:7 that is translated "genea" in the Greek and "relatives" in the English (NAS). "Mispachah" is another Hebrew word found in Jeremiah 8:3 and 10:25 that is translated "genea" in the Greek and "family" in the English (KJ). The Jewish people Jesus was talking to are a people group from the family or relatives of Abraham, Isaac and Jacob. A better understanding might be "THESE PEOPLE AND THEIR RELATIVES WILL BY NO MEANS PASS AWAY TILL ALL THESE THINGS TAKE PLACE" in Mk 13:30 (ET). American Christians—Black and White—would dismiss this question as both irrelevant and unanswerable as the Gospels fail to give us a physical description. The irony is that most of these same Americans in their heart of hearts are pretty confident any way that they know what color Jesus was. They attend churches with images of a tall, long haired, full bearded White man depicted in stained glass windows or painted on walls, and they return home to the same depictions framed in their living room or illustrating their family Bibles. Further compounding the irony is the fact that America actually has an obsession with the (presumed) color of Christ and has exported her White Americanized Savior around the world, as in the book, The Color of Christ: The Son of God and the Saga of Race in America (2012). In fact, the world's most popular and recognizable image of Christ is a distinctly 19th-20th century American creation.

It is true that versions of the "White Christ" appear in European art as early as the 4th century of the Christian era, but these images coexisted with other, nonwhite representations throughout European history. The popularity of the cult of the Black Madonna and Black Christ throughout Europe is evidence of the fact that the European 'White Christ's never acquired the authority and authenticity that the White Christ now has globally. This Christ and his authority are American phenomena. As a predominantly Protestant nation Early America rejected the imaging of Christ that characterized European Catholicism. By the mid-19th century however, in response to American expansion, splintering during the Civil War and subsequent reconstructing, "Whiteness" took on a new significance and a newly- empowered "White Jesus" rose to prominence as the sanctifying symbol of a new national unity and power.

As observed:

"By wrapping itself with the alleged form of Jesus, whiteness gave itself a holy face … With Jesus as white, Americans could feel that sacred whiteness stretched back in time thousands of years and forward in sacred space to heaven and the second coming … The white Jesus promised a white past, a white present, and a future of white glory." As America rose to superpower status in the 20th century she became the world's leading producer and global exporter of White Jesus imagery through film, art, American business, and Christian missions, and has thereby defined the world's view of the Son of God. This globally recognizable Jesus is a totally American product. Indeed, he is an American. Warner Sallman's iconic image of Jesus called Head of Christ (1941) became the most widely reproduced piece of artwork in world history and its depiction the most recognizable face of Jesus in the world. By the 1990s it had been printed over 500 million times and achieved global iconic status. With smooth white skin, long, flowing blondish-brown hair, long beard and blue eyes, this Nordic Christ consciously disguised any hint of Jesus's Semitic, oriental origin—and departed from the older European depictions. It both shaped and was shaped by emerging American ideas of whiteness. The beloved White Jesus of today's world was Made in America.

What, then, did Jesus actually look like? Despite the absence of a detailed description of Jesus's physical appearance in the Gospels (though John the Revelator saw the risen Christ apparently with wooly hair and black feet, Rev. 1:14-15), there are non-biblical evidences that actually allow us to visualize the Son of God from Nazareth. Revelation 1:14-15 – The Kingdom English Standard Bible (TKESB), 14) His head and his hairs were white like wool, as white as snow; and his eyes were as a flame of fire; 15) And his feet like unto fine brass, as if they burned in a furnace; and his voice as the sound of many waters. The first century Jewish writer Josephus (37-100 AD) penned the earliest non-biblical testimony of Jesus. He reportedly had access to official Roman records on which he based his information and in his work Halosis or the "Capture (of Jerusalem)," written around 72 A.D., Josephus discussed "the human form of Jesus and his wonderful works." Unfortunately his texts have passed through Christian hands which altered them, removing offensive material. Fortunately, however, Biblical scholar Robert Eisler in a classic 1931 study of Josephus' Testimony was able to reconstruct the unaltered testimony based on a newly-discovered Old Russian translation that preserved the original Greek text. According to Eisler's reconstruction, the oldest non-Biblical description of Jesus read as follows:

"At that time also there appeared a certain man of magic power … if it be meet to call him a man, [whose name is Jesus], whom [certain] Greeks call a son of [a] God, but his disciples [call] the true prophet … he was a man of simple appearance, mature age, black-skinned (melagchrous), short growth, three cubits tall, hunchbacked, prognathous (lit. 'with a long face' macroprosopos), a long nose, eyebrows meeting above the nose … with scanty curly hair, but having a line in the middle of the head after the fashion of the Nazaraeans, with an undeveloped beard."

This short, black-skinned, mature, hunchbacked Jesus with a unibrow, short curly hair and undeveloped beard bears no resemblance to the Jesus Christ taken for granted today by most of the Christian world: the tall, long haired, long bearded, white-skinned and blue eyed Son of God. Yet, this earliest textual record matches well the earliest iconographic evidence. The earliest visual depiction of Jesus is a painting found in 1921 on a wall of the baptismal chamber of the house-church at Dura Europos, Syria and dated around 235 A.D.

The Jesus that is "Healing the Paralytic Man" (Mark 2:1-12) is short and dark-skinned with a small curly afro - This description has now been supported by the new science of forensic anthropology. In 2002 British forensic scientists and Israeli archaeologists reconstructed what they believe is the most accurate image of Jesus based off of data obtained from the multi-disciplinary approach. In December 2002 Popular Science Magazine published a cover story on the findings which confirm that Jesus would have been short, around 5"1', hair "short with tight curls," a weather-beaten face "which would have made him appear older," dark eyes and complexion: "he probably looked a great deal more like a dark-skinned Semite than Westerners are used to seeing," they concluded. The textual, visual, and scientific evidence agrees, then: Jesus likely was a short, dark-skinned Semite with short curly hair and dark eyes. Colossians 1:15 describes Christ as the "image of the unseen God" and in the Gospel of John (12:45; 14:9) Jesus declares that whoever sees him has seen God. What Jesus "looks like" then is not irrelevant as it is in some way a pointer to God Himself.

The Doctrine of the Great Humility of Christ

From a practical introduction, in the familiar exhortation to follow the example of our Lord, St. Paul passes on to what is, perhaps, the most complete and formal statement in all his Epistles of the doctrine of His "great humility." In this he marks out, first, the Incarnation, in which, "being in the form of God, He took on Him the form of a servant," assuming a sinless but finite humanity; and next, the Passion, which was made needful by the sins of men, and in which His human nature was humiliated to the shame and agony of the cross. Inseparable in themselves, these two great acts of His self-sacrificing love must be distinguished. Ancient speculation delighted to suggest that the first might have been, even if humanity had remained sinless, while the second was added because of the fall and its consequences. Such speculations are, indeed, thoroughly precarious and unsubstantial—for we cannot ask what might have been in a different dispensation from our own; and, moreover, we read of our Lord as "the Lamb slain from the foundation of the world" (Revelation 13:8; 1Peter 1:19)—but they at least point to a true distinction.

As "the Word of God" manifested in the Incarnation, our Lord is the treasure of all humanity as such; as the Savior through death, He is the especial treasure of us as sinners. The purpose of the Apostle in this great passage must ever be kept clearly in view. Our Lord's example is set forth as the pattern of that unselfish disregard of one's own things, and devotion to the things of others, which has just been urged on the Philippians, and the mind which was in Him is presented as the model on which they are to fashion their minds.

This purpose in some measure explains some of the peculiarities of the language here, and may help to guide us through some of the intricacies and doubtful points in the interpretation of the words. It explains why Christ's death is looked at in them only in its bearing upon Himself, as an act of obedience and of condescension, and why even that death in which Jesus stands most inimitable and unique is presented as capable of being imitated by us. The general drift of these verses is clear, but there are few Scripture passages which have evoked more difference of opinion as to the precise meaning of nearly every phrase. To enter on the subtle discussions involved in the adequate exposition of the words would far exceed our limits, and we must perforce content ourselves with a slight treatment of them, and aim chiefly at bringing out their practical side. The broad truth which stands sun-clear amid all diverse interpretations is--that the Incarnation, Life, and Death are the great examples of living humility and self-sacrifice. To be born was His supreme act of condescension. It was love which made Him assume the vesture of human flesh. To die was the climax of His voluntary obedience, and of His devotion to us. The height from which Jesus descended, the whole strange conception of birth as being the voluntary act of the Person born and as being the most stupendous instance of condescension in the world's history, necessarily reposes on the clear conviction that He had a prior existence so lofty that it was an all but infinite descent to become man. Hence Paul begins with the most emphatic assertion that he who bore the name of Jesus lived a divine life before He was born. He uses very strong words which is given in the margin of the Revised Version, and might well have been in its text. 'Being originally' as the word accurately means, carries our thoughts back not only to a state which preceded Bethlehem and the cradle, but to that same timeless eternity from which the prologue of the Gospel of John partially draws the veil when it says, 'In the beginning was the Word,' and to which Jesus.

The Blood of Christ

Himself more obscurely pointed when He said, 'Before Abraham was I am.' Equally emphatic in another direction is Paul's next expression, 'In the form of God,' for 'form' means much more than 'shape.' I would point out the careful selection in this passage of three words to express three ideas which are often by hasty thought regarded as identical. We read of 'the form of God' {verse 6}, 'the likeness of men' {verse 7}, and 'in fashion as a man.' Careful investigation of these two words 'form' and 'fashion' has established a broad distinction between them, the former being more fixed, the latter referring to that which is accidental and outward, which may be fleeting and unsubstantial. The possession of the form involves participation in the essence also. Here it implies no corporeal idea as if God had a material form, but it implies also much more than a mere apparent resemblance. He who is in the form of God possesses the essential divine attributes. Only God can be 'in the form of God': man is made in the likeness of God, but man is not 'in the form of God.' Light is thrown on this lofty phrase by its antithesis with the succeeding expression in the next verse, 'the form of a servant,' and as that is immediately explained to refer to Christ's assumption of human nature, there is no room for candid doubt that 'being originally in the form of God' is a deliberately asserted claim of the divinity of Christ in His pre-existent state. As we have already pointed out, Paul soars here to the same lofty height to which the prologue of John's Gospel rises, and he echoes our Lord's own words about 'the glory which I had with Thee before the foundation of the world.' Our thoughts are carried back before creatures were, and we become dimly aware of an eternal distinction in the divine nature which only perfects its eternal oneness. Such an eternal participation in the divine nature before all creation and before time is the necessary pre-supposition of the worth of Christ's life as the pattern of humility and self-sacrifice. That pre-supposition gives all its meaning, its pathos, and its power, to His gentleness, and love, and death. The facts are different in their significance, and different in their power to bless and gladden, to purge and sway the soul, according as we contemplate them with or without the background of His pre-existent divinity. The view which regards Him as simply a man, like all the rest of us, beginning to be when He was born, takes away from His example its mightiest constraining force.

Only when we with all our hearts believe 'that the Word became flesh,' do we discern the overwhelming depths of condescension manifested in the Birth. If it was not the incarnation of God, it has no claim on the hearts of men. The wondrous act of descent the stages in that long descent are marked out with precision and definiteness which would be intolerable presumption, if Paul were speaking only his thoughts, or telling what he had seen with his own eyes. They begin with what was in the mind of the eternal Word before He began His descent and whilst yet He is 'in the form of God.' He stands on the lofty level before the descent begins, and in spirit makes the surrender, which, stage by stage, is afterwards to be wrought out in act. Before any of these acts there must have been the disposition of mind and will which Paul describes as 'counting it not a thing to be grasped to be on equality with God.' He did not regard the being equal to God as a prey or treasure to be clutched and retained at all hazards. That sweeps our thoughts into the dim regions far beyond Calvary or Bethlehem, and is a more overwhelming manifestation of love than are the acts of lowly gentleness and patient endurance which followed in time. It included and transcended them all. It was the supreme example of not 'looking on one's own things.' And what made Him so count? What but infinite love. To rescue men, and win them to Himself and goodness, and finally to lift them to the place from which He came down for them, seemed to Him to be worth the temporary surrender of that glory and majesty. We can but bow and adore the perfect love. We look more deeply into the depths of Deity than unaided eyes could ever penetrate, and what we see is the movement in that abyss of Godhead of purest surrender which, by beholding, we are to assimilate. Then comes the wonder of wonders, 'He emptied Himself.' We cannot enter here on the questions which gather round that phrase, and which give it a factitious importance in regard to present controversies. All that we would point out now is that while the Apostle distinctly treats the Incarnation as being a laying aside of what made the Word to be equal with God, he says nothing, on which an exact determination can be based, of the degree or particulars in which the divine nature of our Lord was limited by His humanity. The fact he asserts, and that is all. The scene in the Upper Chamber was but a feeble picture of what had already been done behind the veil. Unless He had laid aside His garments of divine glory and majesty, He would have had no human flesh from which to strip the robes. Unless He had willed to take the 'form of a servant,' He would not have had a body to gird with the slave's towel.

The Incarnation, which made all His acts of lowly love possible, was a greater act of lowly love than those which flowed from it. Looking at it from earth, men say, 'Jesus was born.' Looking at it from heaven, Angels say, He emptied Himself. But how did He empty Himself? By taking the form of a slave, that is to God. And how did He take the form of a slave? By becoming in the likeness of men. Here we are specially to note the remarkable language implying that what is true of none other in all the generations of men is true of Him. That just as 'emptying Himself' was His own act, also the taking the form of a slave by His being born was His own act, and was more truly described as a 'becoming.' We note, too, the strong contrast between that most remarkable word and the 'being originally' which is used to express the mystery of divine pre-existence. Whilst His becoming in the likeness of men stands in strong contrast with 'being originally' and energetically expresses the voluntariness of our Lord's birth, the 'likeness of men' does not cast any doubt on the reality of His manhood, but points to the fact that though certainly perfect man He was by reason of the divine nature present in Him not simply and merely man. Here then the beginning of Christ's manhood is spoken of in terms which are only explicable, if it was a second form of being, preceded by a pre-existent form, and was assumed by His own act. The language, too, demands that that humanity should have been true essential manhood. It was in 'the form' of man and possessed of all essential attributes. It was in 'the likenesses of man possessed of all external characteristics and yet was something more. It summed up human nature and was its representative as well. The obedience which attended the descent, it was not merely an act of humiliation and condescension to become man, but all His life was one long act of lowliness. Just as He 'emptied Himself' in the act of becoming in the 'likeness of men,' so He 'humbled Himself,' and all along the course of His earthly life He chose constant lowliness and to be 'despised and rejected of men.' It was the result moment by moment of His own will that to the eyes of men He presented 'no form nor comeliness,' and that will was moment by moment steadied in its unmoved humility, because He perpetually looked 'not on His own things, but on the things of others.' The guise He presented to the eyes of men was 'the fashion of a man.' That word corresponds exactly to Paul's carefully selected term, and makes emphatic both its superficial and its transitory character.

The lifelong humbling of Himself was further manifested in His becoming 'obedient.' That obedience was, of course, to God. And here we cannot but pause to ask the question, How comes it that to the man Jesus obedience to God was an act of humiliation? Surely there is but one explanation of such a statement. For all men but this one to be God's slaves is their highest honor, and to speak of obedience as humiliation is a sheer absurdity. Not only was the life of Jesus so perfect an example of unbroken obedience that He could safely front His adversaries with the question, 'Which of you convinced Me of sin?' and with the claim to 'do always the things that pleased Him,' but the obedience to the Father was perfected in His death. Consider the extraordinary fact that a man's death is the crowning instance of his humility, and ask yourselves the question, Who then is this who chose to be born, and stooped in the act of dying? His death was obedience to God, because by it He carried out the Father's will for the salvation of the world, His death is the greatest instance of unselfish self-sacrifice, and the loftiest example of looking on the 'things of others' that the world has ever seen. It dwindles in significance, in pathos, and in power to move us to imitation unless we clearly see the divine glory of the eternal Lord as the background of the gentle lowliness of the Man of Sorrows, and the Cross. No theory of Christ's life and death but that He was born for us, and died for us, either explains the facts and the apostolic language concerning them, or leaves them invested with their full power to melt our hearts and mould our lives. There is a possibility of imitating Him in the most transcendent of His acts. The mind may be in us which was in Christ Jesus. That it may, His death must first be the ground of our hope, and then we must make it the pattern of our lives, and draw from it the power to shape them after His blessed Example. Php 2:5-6. Let this mind — The same humble, condescending, benevolent, disinterested, self-denying disposition; be in you which was also in Christ Jesus — The original expression, τουτο φρονεισθω εν υμιν ο και εν Χριστω Ιησου, is, literally, Be you minded, or disposed, as Jesus was. The word includes mind and heart, the understanding, will, and affections. Let your judgment and estimation of things, your choice, desire, intention, determination, and subsequent practice, be like those in him; who being — Υπαρχων, subsisting; in the form of God — As having been from eternity possessed of divine perfections and glories; thought it not robbery — Greek, ουκ αρπαγμον ηγησατο; literally, did not consider it an act of robbery, ειναι ισα Θεω, to be equal things with God —

He and his Father being one, John 10:30; and all things belonging to the Father being his, John 16:15; the Father also being in him, and he in the Father. Accordingly, the highest divine names, titles, attributes, and works, are inscribed to him by the inspired writers: and the same honors and adorations are represented as being due to him, and are actually paid to him, which are given to the Father, and to the Holy Spirit. "As the apostle," says thelogians, "is here speaking of what Christ was before he took the form of a servant, the form of God, in which he is said to have subsisted, and of which he is said (Php 2:7) to have divested himself when he became man, cannot be anything which he possessed during his incarnation, or in his divested state; consequently, neither Erasmus's opinion, that the form of God consisted in those sparks of divinity by which Christ, during his incarnation, manifested his Godhead; nor the opinion of the Socinians, that it consisted in the power of working miracles, is well founded." The opinion of others, "seems better founded, who, by the form of God, understand that visible glorious light in which the Deity is said to dwell, 1 Timothy 6:16; and by which he manifested himself to the patriarchs of old, Deuteronomy 5:22; Deuteronomy 5:24; and which was commonly accompanied with a numerous retinue of angels, Psalm 68:17; and which in Scripture is called the similitude, Numbers 12:8; the face, Psalm 31:10; the presence, Exodus 33:15; and the shape (John 5:37) of God. This interpretation is supported by the term μορφη, forms, here used, which signifies a person's external shape or appearance.

Thus we are told (Mark 16:12) that Jesus appeared to his disciples in another μορφη, shape, or form: and Matthew 17:2, Μεταμορφωθη, He was transfigured before them; his outward appearance or form was changed. Further, this interpretation agrees with the fact. The form of God, that is, the visible glory, and the attendance of angels above described, the Son of God enjoyed with his Father before the world was, John 17:5; and on that, as on other accounts, he is the brightness of the Father's glory, Hebrews 1:3. But he divested himself thereof when he became flesh. However, having resumed it after his ascension, he will come with it in the human nature to judge the world. So he told his disciples, Matthew 16:27. Lastly, this sense of μορφη Θεου, is confirmed by the meaning of μορφην δουλου, (Php 2:7,) which evidently denotes the appearance and behavior of a servant,"2:5-11. The example of the Lord Jesus Christ is set before Christians.

We must resemble him in his life, if we would have the benefit of his death. Notice the two natures of Christ; his Divine nature, and human nature. Who being in the form of God, partaking the Divine nature, as the eternal and only begotten Son of God, John 1:1, had not thought it a robbery to be equal with God, and to receive Divine worship from men. His human nature; herein he became like us in all things except sin. Thus low, of his own will, he stooped from the glory he had with the Father before the world was. Christ's two states, of humiliation and exaltation, are noticed. Christ not only took upon him the likeness and fashion, or form of a man, but of one in a low state; not appearing in splendor. His whole life was a life of poverty and suffering. But the lowest step was his dying the death of the cross, the death of a malefactor and a slave; exposed to public hatred and scorn. The exaltation was of Christ's human nature, in union with the Divine. At the name of Jesus, not the mere sound of the word, but the authority of Jesus, all should pay solemn homage. It is to the glory of God the Father, to confess that Jesus Christ is Lord; for it is his will, that all men should honor the Son as they honor the Father, John 5:23. Here we see such motives to self-denying love as nothing else can supply. Do we thus love and obey the Son of God? Let this mind be in you, which was also in Christ Jesus; The object of this reference to the example of the Savior is particularly to enforce the duty of humility. This was the highest example which could be furnished, and it would illustrate and confirm all the apostle had said of this virtue. The principle in the case is, that we are to make the Lord Jesus our model, and are in all respects to frame our lives, as far as possible, in accordance with this great example. The point here is, that he left a state of inexpressible glory, and took upon him the most humble form of humanity, and performed the lowly offices, that he might benefit us. The oldest manuscripts read, "Have this mind in you." He does not put forward himself (Php 2:4, and Php 1:24) as an example, but Christ, THE ONE pre-eminently who sought not His own, but "humbled Himself" (Php 2:8), first in taking on Him our nature, secondly, in humbling Himself further in that nature (Ro 15:3). Let this mind be in you,....The Arabic version renders it, "let that humility be perceived in you". The apostle proposes Christ as the great pattern and exemplar of humility and instances in his assumption of human nature and in his subjection to all that meanness, and death itself, even the death of the cross in it and which he mentions with this view, to engage the saints to lowliness of mind in imitation of him;

to show forth the same temper and disposition of mind in their practice which also was in Christ Jesus; or as the Syriac version, "think ye the same thing as Jesus Christ"; let the same condescending spirit and humble deportment appear in you as in him. This mind, affection, and conduct of Christ, may refer both to his early affection to his people, the love he bore to them from everlasting, the resolution and determination of his mind in consequence of it; and his agreement with his Father to take upon him their nature in the fullness of time and to do his will by obeying, suffering, and dying in their room and stead and also the open exhibition and execution of all this in time, when he appeared in human nature, poor, mean, and abject; condescending to the lowest offices, and behaving in the most meek and humble manner, throughout the whole of his life, to the moment of his death.

Let this mind be in you, which was also in Christ Jesus:

He sets before them a most perfect example of all modesty and sweet conduct, Christ Jesus, whom we ought to follow with all our might: who abased himself so much for our sakes, although he is above all, that he took upon himself the form of a servant, that is, our flesh, willingly subject to all weaknesses, even to the death of the cross. "Christianity without Christ is no Christianity; and a Christ not Divine is one other than the Christ on whom the souls of Christians have habitually fed. What virtue, what piety, have existed outside of Christianity, is a question totally distinct. But to hold that, since the great controversy of the early time was wound up at Chalcedon, the question of our Lord's Divinity has generated all the storms of the Christian atmosphere would be simply an historical untruth. "Christianity … produced a type of character wholly new to the Roman world, and it fundamentally altered the laws and institutions, the tone, temper and tradition of that world. For example, it changed profoundly the relation of the poor to the rich … It abolished slavery, and a multitude of other horrors. It restored the position of woman in society. It made peace, instead of war, the normal and presumed relation between human societies. It exhibited life as a discipline … in all its parts, and changed essentially the place and function of suffering in human experience … All this has been done not by eclectic and arbitrary fancies, but by the creed of the Homoousion, (Christ is of one substance with God) in which the philosophy of modern times sometimes appears to find a favorite theme of ridicule.

The whole fabric, social as well as personal, rests on the new type of character which the Gospel brought into life and action." "He was found in fashion as a man: it was a wonderful discovery, an astonishing spectacle in the view of angels, that He who was in the form of God, and adored from eternity, should be made in fashion as a man. But why is it not said that He was a man?

For the same reason that the Apostle wishes to dwell upon the appearance of our Savior, not as excluding the reality but as exemplifying His condescension. His being in the form of God did not prove that He was not God, but rather that He was God, and entitled to supreme honor. So, His assuming the form of a servant and being in the likeness of man, does not prove that He was not man, but, on the contrary, includes it; at the same time including a manifestation of Himself, agreeably to His design of purchasing the salvation of His people, and dying for the sins of the world, by sacrificing Himself upon the Cross." The best refutation of such expositions is the repeated perusal of the Epistle itself, with its noon-day practicality of precept and purity of affections, and not least its high language about the sanctity of the body—an idea wholly foreign to the Gnostic sphere of thought that supposed the passage Php 3:1 to Php 4:9 to be an interpolation. But, not to speak of the total absence of any historical or documentary support for such a theory, the careful reader will find in that section just those minute touches of harmony with the rest of the Epistle, e.g. in the indicated need of internal union at Philippi, which are the surest signs of homogeneity. The appeal enforced by the supreme Example of the Savior in His Incarnation, Obedience and Exaltation. Paul also was one who had regard to what belonged to others, not merely what belonged to himself Php 1:24 : and this circumstance furnished him with the occasion of this admonition.

He does not, however, propose himself, but Christ, as an example, who did not seek His own, but humbled Himself. [Even the very order of the words, as the name Christ is put first, indicates the immense weight of this example. Verse 5. - Let this mind be in you, which was also in Christ Jesus; literally, according to the reading of the best manuscripts, mind this in you which was also (minded) in Christ Jesus. Many manuscripts take the words "every man" (ἕκαστοι) of Ver. 4 with Ver. 5: "All of you mind this."

The words, "in Christ Jesus," show that the corresponding words, "in you," cannot mean "among you," but in yourselves, in your heart. The apostle refers us to the supreme example of unselfishness and humility, the Lord Jesus Christ. He bids us mind (comp. Romans 8:5) the things which the Lord Jesus minded, to love what he loved, to hate what he hated; the thoughts, desires, motives, of the Christian should be the thoughts, desires, motives, which filled the sacred heart of a Jesus Christ. Christians will strive to imitate him, to reproduce his image, not only in the outward, but even in the inner life. Especially being bidden to follow the unselfishness and humility ways the written word portrays him.

CHAPTER VII

Jesus Bar-Abbas(Son Of The Father)

JESUS BAR ABBAS

Just before Jesus is handed over to be crucified, Pontius Pilate presents the crowds with the choice to release one of two prisoners. The first is described as 'a notorious prisoner' (Matthew 27:16), 'someone who had committed murder in the insurrection' (Mark 15:7), while Pilate knows full well that the second, Jesus, had been handed over in envy.

Two options for the first prisoner's name are visible in popular modern translations of Matthew 27:16–17:

ESV: And they had then a notorious prisoner called Barabbas. So when they had gathered, Pilate said to them, "Whom do you want me to release for you: Barabbas, or Jesus who is called Christ?"

NIV: At that time they had a well-known prisoner whose name was Jesus Barabbas. So when the crowd had gathered, Pilate asked them, "Which one do you want me to release to you: Jesus Barabbas, or Jesus who is called the Messiah?"

A few Greek manuscripts do have this expanded name for Barabbas in Matthew 27:16–17, namely Jesus Barabbas instead of simply 'Barabbas'. Of course, this longer name heightens the dramatic contrast, 'Who do you want me to release to you, Jesus Barabbas or Jesus who is called Christ?' The crowd has a choice between two Jesus, one arrested for murder, and the other, the son of God.

Despite the obvious preach ability of this textual variant, it is unlikely to be what Matthew originally wrote. The variant has limited support in the surviving manuscripts of the New Testament; none of the manuscripts that have the name 'Jesus Barabbas' come from before the tenth century. However, a closer look at the full evidence shows that the variant has an impressive pedigree and goes back a long way in church history.

The most direct evidence for the variant comes from a manuscript written not in Greek, but in Syriac, located in St Catherine's monastery on Mt Sinai, and was first identified by the Scottish biblical scholars, Agnes Smith Lewis and Margaret Dunlop Gibson, in the late nineteenth century. This manuscript is a palimpsest, meaning that the parchment of the original text (the four Gospels in Syriac) was later re-used and overwritten with a different text. The older, underlying text of the manuscript which testifies to the name 'Jesus Barabbas' may come from as early as the fifth century—five centuries before the earliest attestation in a Greek Gospel manuscript. So in this Syriac translation we have evidence that the alternative reading was perhaps more widely known than our tenth century Gospel manuscripts would suggest. To date there is no other direct manuscript evidence in any other language of Barabbas being called 'Jesus Barabbas', yet there is more evidence to take into consideration.

There is a Gospel manuscript written in majuscule letters (in contrast to the more common minuscule script its found in most New Testament manuscripts) from the tenth century that contains about a dozen or so marginal comments spread out across the four Gospels These comments betray a historical interest in certain people that are mentioned. So for example, next to the genealogy of Jesus in Matthew it explains how Jesus' ancestor Matthan (Hebrew name Mattan, which means "gift") is the link between Mary and Elisabeth (Matthew 1:15). At Matthew 27 it has a note that starts like this:

"But in very old copies I encountered, I found also Barabbas called Jesus. So therefore the question of Pilate is there, 'whom do you wish from the two that I release to you? Jesus Barabbas or Jesus who is called Christ?' For it seems that the patronym of the robber was Barabbas, which is interpreted as 'son of the teacher.'"

Instead of assuming a text that has Jesus Barabbas as the variant, it comments from the perspective that 'Jesus Barabbas' is the main text, and just 'Barabbas' is the variant. Whichever way it appeared in Origen's original commentary in Greek, it is clear that the variant 'Jesus Barabbas' goes all the way back into the third century, and that much later manuscripts did preserve an old, though incorrect, reading.

So where did it come from? How did such a strange error come into being? In the nineteenth century, the biblical scholar, Samuel Prideaux Tregelles, offered the most probable explanation. He noticed that in Matthew 27:17, in the clause, 'Who do you want me to release to you, Barabbas or Jesus' the last two letters of 'to you' form the standard abbreviation used for 'Jesus'. The name 'Jesus' was one of the words consistently abbreviated by writing only the first and last letter(s), one of the so-called nomina sacra. A scribe, in anticipation of the name Jesus, could easily have been tricked into reading the final letters of ('to you') twice, leading to a text that reads:

If this explanation is correct, it would mean that all the confusion that left its traces for at least 700 years and longer in the manuscript tradition goes back to a simple, common copying error.

So what do we do when modern Bible translations reproduce copying errors? Firstly, we can be encouraged that Bible translation is a work in progress. Translations like the NIV and ESV need periodic updates because of the knowledge becomes more precise. They are the careful work of teams of scholars who scrutinize many suggested changes to the text. Secondly, one can be encouraged that this process is not concealed from view. It is no secret that the ESV and NIV render these verses differently, or which manuscripts each reading relies on. The problem is mentioned in the footnotes. We are fortunate enough to have a variety of modern translations at our fingertips and can easily compare the different conclusions formed by the translation committees.

Thirdly, we can be encouraged and compelled by the reminder of how the Bible's text has been transmitted through the centuries. Thanks to the surviving manuscript evidence we can be confident in the text of the New Testament. We can make detailed investigations into individual words in these manuscripts, and in the majority of cases, we can recover the exact words New Testament authors wrote. There is a textual problem in Matt 27:16 & 17 as to whether the name of the criminal was just "Barabbas" or "Jesus Barabbas". The USB5(the Greek New Testament) regards the most probable reading as "Jesus Barabbas" but is far from certain.

Let's assume that the correct text is "Jesus Barabbas". The irony of the choice between "Jesus Barabbas the Son of the Father " and "Jesus Christ the one they call the Messiah" is total.

JESUS

"Jesus" is the Greek transliteration of the Hebrew "Joshua" which means "the LORD is salvation", or "The LORD saves". There is a direct reference to this in Matt 1:21; She will give birth to a Son, and you are to give Him the name Jesus because He will save His people from their sins."

BAR ABBAS

Bar Abbas is Aramaic for "Son of the Father".

CHRIST or MESSIAH

Christ is Greek for "anointed one". The word "Messiah" is Hebrew with the same meaning. The Irony, Pilate was no fool and understood this well and mocked the Jews by putting a stark question to them:

Do you want me to release to you either:

Jesus Barabbas [The savior who is the son of the father] and a criminal who had been involved in a political insurrection, John 18:40. Jesus Christ [The Savior who is the Anointed One, who is called the Messiah] a man (John 19:5) who was holy, innocent, blameless, set apart from sinners (Heb 7:26). To complete the irony, Pilate set a sign over the cross.
Pilate also had a notice posted on the cross. It read: JESUS OF NAZARETH, THE KING OF THE JEWS. (John 19:19). Thus, when the Jews insisted that Jesus Barabbas(Bar Abbas) to be released and Jesus(The one they call the Messiah) be crucified Did they selected a false messiah and crucified the true Messiah? Indeed, Barabbas (meaning "son of the father") has the given name "Jesus" and this historical person has present-day implications as many come preaching "another Jesus" today….a "Jesus" that is the "son" of a church father…or maybe the son of the father of the lie….and is not the true Son of the Father.

Jesus Bar-Abbas(Son Of The Father)

2 Corinthians 11:3-4 But I fear, lest by any means, as the serpent beguiled Eve through his subtilty, so your minds should be corrupted from the simplicity that is in Christ. For if he that comes to preach another Jesus, whom we have not preached, or if you receive another spirit, which you have not received, or another gospel, which you have not accepted, you might well bear with him.

There are 2 Jesus being presented here: Jesus Barabbas (the son of the Father) and Jesus the one being called "Christ" (Anointed) who is the Son of the Father in Heaven.

Matthew 27:16-17 (16) And they had then a notable prisoner, called Jesus Bar Abbas. (17) Therefore when they were gathered together, Pilate said unto them, Whom will you that I release unto you? Jesus Bar Abbas, or Jesus which is called the Messiah?

The choosing between the 2 called "Jesus" has not ceased today as there are many who come to us preaching about "Jesus" But rather knowing who the true Jesus is being called Christ or to choose the "Jesus Bar Abbas", choose the one they are preaching about who was "crucified" choose the true Jesus whose name mean "Son Of The Father? Our own eternal life do not appears outwardly, in our mortal flesh. It's the inward spirit that rules.

According to the written word, it was the "chief priests and elders" who wanted the multitude to choose the Jesus Bar Abbas…the son of the Father… and destroy the Son (Jesus) who is called the Messiah. They used persuasive words (convincing words that seemed true to the multitude's hearing) But still to this day as the world chooses their "Jesus Christ" the one they call the Messiah. In the face of preaching Jesus Christ (European name Cesare Borgia) rather than the Jesus with:
 Rev, 1:16,17… hair on his head was white like wool, as white as snow, and his eyes were like blazing fire. 15His feet were like bronze glowing in a furnace, and his voice was like the sound of rushing waters. .

Matthew 27:20-22 (20) But the chief priests and elders persuaded the multitude that they should ask Jesus Barabbas(Bar Abbas), and destroy Jesus Christ. (21) "Which of the two do you want me to release to you?" asked the governor.. "Barabbas," they answered.

(22) "What shall I do, then, with Jesus who is called the Messiah?" Pilate asked. They all answered, "Crucify him!"

Paul calls them the "very chiefest apostles" who come forth to us today to preach "another Jesus" than the One that the apostles preach (Jesus Christ). The apostles preached Jesus Christ and not "Jesus Bar Abbas" the son of the Father or did scribe who wrote a handwritten word of church dogmas for us to keep in order to serve their "White Jesus". The Roman centurion Lucius entered the cell in which Jesus Barabbas was imprisoned. "Do you know the man named Jesus from Nazareth?" Lucius asked.

"I know the man," Jesus Barabbas said.

"Does he deserve to die?"

"No more than I!" Jesus Barabbas shouted in a near rage.

Lucius approached Jesus Barabbas and began to unlock his shackles. ``You compare yourself in the same breath . . . ?" Lucius said, disgusted.

"We both seek the same thing-FREEDOM!!" Jesus Barabbas bellowed defiantly. ``Only our methods differ!"

Lucius looked doubtfully upon Jesus Barabbas. "The freedom he spoke of is not the same you kill for," he said.

After an uncomfortable silence as Lucius continued loosing the shackles, Jesus Barabbas asked, ``When is the man Jesus to die?"

"He carries his cross now," Lucius said.

Freed from his chains, Barabbas backed hastily away, and said in a tone partly defiant, partly fearful and accusing, "Now why do you tell me all this? Why don't you take me with him-get it over with?"

"Go!" Lucius ordered. "You're free. The man Jesus is dying in your place. One prisoner is freed each year at this time. Pilate offered that mob a choice," he explained.

Jesus Bar-Abbas(Son Of The Father)

"Me? They chose me?" Jesus Barabbas said, filling with a mix of gratitude, astonishment, and self-importance.

``Your followers yelled the loudest," Lucius said.

Such was the dramatisation of the freeing of Barabbas in 1961 classic King of Kings, a movie in which Barabbas is almost as central to the plot as Jesus is. Indeed, at times the Barabbas of King of Kings overshadows Jesus, especially during the two lengthy scenes of dramatic battle between the forces of Barabbas the Freedom-Fighter and the Roman armies in Judaea and Jerusalem.

In stark contrast, Mel Gibson's The Passion of the Christ shows us a Jesus Barabbas who is thoroughly repugnant in appearance and demeanor, a wretched man perhaps suffering from a mental illness, perhaps a psychotic serial killer-a social outcast certainly no rebel warrior struggling to liberate his people from Roman rule.

So, was the movie King of King's Barabbas the more accurate depiction, or was Gibson's? The only historical documents that have anything to say about Barabbas is that of the four Gospels and the Acts of the Apostles in the New Testament. The biblical texts in modern English version, the New American Bible:

Now on the occasion of the feast the governor was accustomed to release to the crowd one prisoner whom they wished. And at that time they had a notorious prisoner called [Jesus] Barabbas. So when they had assembled, Pilate said to them, 'Which one do you want me to release to you, [Jesus] Barabbas, or Jesus called Messiah?' For he knew that it was out of envy that they had handed him over. . . . The chief priests and the elders persuaded the crowds to ask for Barabbas but to destroy Jesus. The governor said to them in reply, `Which of the two do you want me to release to you?' They answered, `Barabbas!' . . . . Then he released Barabbas to them, ..." (Matt. 27:15-18, 20-21, 26)

``Now on the occasion of the feast he used to release to them one prisoner whom they requested. A man called Jesus Barabbas was then in prison along with the rebels who had committed murder in a rebellion(during the Roman invasion).

The crowd came forward and began to ask him to do for them as he was accustomed. Pilate answered, `Do you want me to release to you the king of the Jews?'

For he knew that it was out of envy that the chief priests had handed him over. But the chief priests stirred up the crowd to have him release Barabbas for them instead. . . . So Pilate, wishing to satisfy the crowd, released Barabbas to them . . . ." (Mark 15:6-11, 15)

[He was obliged to release one prisoner for them at the festival.] But all together they shouted out, `Away with this man! Release Barabbas to us.' (Now Barabbas had been imprisoned for a rebellion that had taken place in the city and for murder.) . . . . So he released the man who had been imprisoned for rebellion and murder, for whom they asked . . . ." (Luke 23:18, 25)

When he had said this, he again went out to the Jews and said to them, `I find no guilt in him. But you have a custom that I release one prisoner to you at Passover. Do you want me to release to you the King of the Jews?' They cried out again, `Not this one but Barabbas!' Now Barabbas was a revolutionary." (John 18:38-40)

You denied the Holy and Righteous One and asked that a murderer be released to you." (Acts 3:14)

Judging from the way the New American Bible renders these passages, Bar Abbas would obviously be much more historically accurate than, when words such as a rebellion," the rebels," and a revolutionary." But when you look a little closer, serious problems arise with the picture of "Jesus Barabbas(Bar Abbas), (Son of the Father) as a Freedom-Fighter."

Perhaps the most serious problem is that it is virtually impossible that Pilate would agree to release a dangerous revolutionary and menace to Roman authority as Barabbas is supposed to have been. The Gospels say that Pilate gave the crowd a choice between Jesus and Barabbas. But what Roman procurator in his right mind would give such a choice? Were there no other notable prisoners that Pilate could have offered them? This consideration is especially important when we remember that Pilate wanted to release Jesus.

The implication is that he offered them Jesus Barabbas because he believed that, if offered a choice, they would surely choose Jesus instead of Barabbas. That suggests Barabbas was not a well-liked man either among the Jews or the Roman authorities.

Indeed, the Gospels say Jesus Barabbas was guilty of murder, and Matthew calls him notorious, not a descriptions one would expect to find attached to a heroic Freedom-Fighter at least not one who was popular. If Barabbas really was a dangerous revolutionary, we have every reason to believe it was not in Pilate's interest to offer to release him. Something here don't add up.

To unravel this knot, take another look at the biblical testimony. John's parenthetical statement identifying Jesus Barabbas. Now Jesus Barabbas was a revolutionary. The New American Standard Bible has John saying. The Greek word rendered "revolutionary" is leistes, which appears in three other important places in the Gospels. In Matt. 27:38 and Mark 15:27, it is the word used for the two men who were crucified with Jesus. In Luke 22:52, Jesus asks the men who had come to arrest Him, ``Have you come out as against a leistes, with swords and clubs?'' In Luke 10:30, in the Parable of the Good Samaritan, it is the word used for those who brutally attacked the man whom the Good Samaritan would help.

Interestingly enough, in Matt. 27:38 and Mark 15:27, the New American Standard Bible says that the two men crucified with Jesus Christ were not "thieves" or "robbers" as Christians have believed for centuries upon centuries but revolutionaries, which agrees with the New American Bible's rendering of John 18:40. However, in Luke 10:30 and Luke 22:52, the New American Standard Bible inconsistently refers to "robbers," not "revolutionaries" but then perhaps the translators were sympathetic to leftist revolution and didn't want to have the world to read, Jesus talk of a man being robbed and nearly beaten to death by ``revolutionaries''?

 Although, the written word New Testament says leistes comes from a Greek masculine noun meaning "to plunder," or "a robber; bandit, brigand." Nothing is said about "revolutionary" as a possible meaning of leistes. 2).In the scripture passage discussion, the King James Version translates leistes as either "thief" or "robber," while the Douay-Rheims-Confraternity Version consistently renders it "a robber" in these verses.

If Jesus Barabbas was a revolutionary as the New American Standard Bible claims, then Jesus Barabbas is the more historically accurate, but if he was a "robber" or "brigand," as the original Greek indicates, then Jesus Barabbas is the Son Of The Father. Because the real question is as Jesus Christ was nailed to the cross and two others along with him. The two were called robber(Jesus Bar Abbas) and a murder(Jesus Bar Abbas) But yet Jesus Barabbas was set free never spoken of in that part of the written word again. I t was like his character just vanished out from the scene. So how about Jesus Bar Abbas(Son Of the father) put on the cross next to Jesus Christ in the written word of the Greek New Testament as a allegory fact, that they are technically the same person.

Incidentally, the 1961 movie King of Kings stuck with ancient tradition by identifying the criminals who were crucified with Jesus as ``thieves" rather than revolutionaries: "We are only thieves," one of them says to Jesus Barabbas. "You're a murderer!" (In fact they were "robbers," not just ``thieves" men who had committed murder as well as theft, hence their death sentences.) But there seem to be an identity of the two as thieves or Jesus Bar Abbas(Son Of The Father), the Hebrew meaning, the Greek meaning is Son Of A teacher or Church father to make lite of keeping the white Jesus intact for the spell bounding practices of the Christian(Greek term Cretan… meaning stupid people).

But what of the Gospels, references to that "rebellion" in Jerusalem in which Jesus Barabbas and others had participated, during which Jesus Bar Abbas had committed murder? Surely that would indicate that Jesus Bar Abbas was some sort of militant rebel against Rome?

The Greek word translated "rebellion" is stasis, meaning "insurrection," and "strife, dissension." Thus, "rebellion" is indeed a possible translation. However, another acceptable translation would be "riot" or "civil disturbance" or "mob action," as the Douay-Rheims-Confraternity Version indicates. Similarly, the "rebels" who were arrested along with Jesus Bar Abbas may just have been "rioters", the Greek word means someone who had participated in a stasis. If the Gospels were referring to a "rebellion" in Jerusalem, then Barabbas could theoretically have been an outlaw Freedom Fighter.

However, the fact that the Bible calls Jesus Barabbas a "robber" and "murderer" makes things interesting. There's simply no good reason to believe that Jesus Barabbas(Son Of the Father) had either instigated or participated in a formal rebellion in Jerusalem. Rather, it seems likely that he was a common thug and highway robber who became ``notorious'' when the so call murdered of one or more persons during a riot or mob action in Jerusalem. When considering Pilate's motive for offering the crowds a choice between Jesus Christ and Jesus Bar Abbas, you are led to conclude that Pilate thought the people of Jerusalem would never want someone like Jesus Barabbas to be spared the death penalty, which is consistent with a Jesus Barabbas who was a violent criminal but not with a Jesus Barabbas who was a rebel against Rome. As stated, Pilate would never consider amnesty for an enemy of Rome just to find a way t! to free a man he knew was not guilty of the accusations the chief priests had leveled against Him, but Pilate might have consider a level of amnesty for a notorious violent criminal in such circumstances.

So it turns out that Jesus Bar Abbas(Son Of the Father) actually and allegorically is the same as Jesus the one they call the Messiah . Though recent biblical studies have done much to increase our understanding of the written word, the Jesus Barabbas as Freedom-Fighter" theory is one of several examples of modern biblical scholarship that fails to stand up to recognize that Jesus Bar Abbas(Son Of The Father) the rebel is no different than Jesus Christ(the one they call the Messiah) who went into the market place with a bull whip and began to beat and destroy the market activity as well as the whooping the people for their money hungry foolishness. You have to read between the lines Both on trial, one seem to be released from trial as a thief and a murderer, the other subjected to death on the cross, but two unknown persons(Jesus Bar Abbas a thief and a murderer) later known as a thief and a murderer nail to a cross as well. Think about that, take time and THINK!!!

IT'S WONDERFUL WHEN YOU CAN COLLABORATE AND COOPERATE WITH OTHERS, MAKING CONTRIBUTIONS AND RECEIVING BENEFITS FROM A LARGER COMMUNITY. YET IN ORDER TO DO SO, AT THE END OF THE DAY YOU MUST BE ABLE TO RELY ON YOURSELF. EMBRACE THE OPPORTUNITIES TO STRENGTHEN AND IMPROVE YOURSELF, FROM YOUR LOWER CONSCIOUSNESS TO YOUR HIGHER CONSCIOUSNESS. THE BEST THING YOU CAN DO FOR YOU IS TO CONTINUE REACHING FOR THE NEXT LEVEL OF YOUR LIFE.

— *Dr. Anthony Martin*